AF760862

PROFITS, WAGES, AND PRODUCTIVITY IN THE BUSINESS CYCLE

PROFITS, WAGES, AND PRODUCTIVITY IN THE BUSINESS CYCLE

A KALDORIAN ANALYSIS

MITSUHIKO IYODA
Momoyama Gakuin Daigaku Osaka, Japan

KLUWER ACADEMIC PUBLISHERS
BOSTON/DORDRECHT/LONDON

Distributors for North America:
Kluwer Academic Publishers
101 Philip Drive
Assinippi Park
Norwell, Massachusetts 02061 USA

Distributors for all other countries:
Kluwer Academic Publishers Group
Distribution Centre
Post Office Box 322
3300 AH Dordrecht, THE NETHERLANDS

Library of Congress Cataloging-in-Publication Data
Iyoda, Mitsuhiko, 1943–
Profits, wages, and productivity in the business cycle : a Kaldorian analysis / by Mitsuhiko Iyoda.
p. cm.
Originally presented as the author's thesis (doctoral)—University of Buckingham, 1994.
Includes bibliographical references and index.
ISBN 0–7923–9868–8 (alk. paper)
1. Business cycles. 2. Income distribution. 3. Kaldor, Nicholas, 1908–1986. I. Title.
HB3714.I95 1997
338.5′42—dc21 96–40418
CIP

Copyright © 1997 by Kluwer Academic Publishers

All rights reserved. No part of this publication may be reproduced, stored in a retrieval system or transmitted in any form or by any means, mechanical, photo-copying, recording, or otherwise, without the prior written permission of the publisher, Kluwer Academic Publishers, 101 Philip Drive, Assinippi Park, Norwell, Massachusetts 02061.

Printed on acid-free paper.

Printed in the United States of America

CONTENTS

LIST OF FIGURES

LIST OF TABLES

PREFACE

This book attempts to explain the changes in specific macroeconomic variables—such as the relative share of labor, the profit rate, and the real wage rate in advanced capitalist economies—in relation to the influence of the business cycle in income distribution.

In the pursuit of this inquiry, I first establish some stylized facts that I wish to investigate. The three countries discussed here—the United Kingdom, the United States, and Japan—are observed over a period of twenty-two years beginning in 1970, which covers at least three business cycles.

This study makes several assumptions. First, there is no common feature on whether labor share moves countercyclically or procyclically; however, labor share increases in the first year of contraction and decreases in the first year of expansion, though there are some exceptions. Second, the profit rate moves procyclically. Third, labor productivity moves procyclically and shows a symmetrical change; productivity sharply increases in the first year of expansion in terms of the growth rate and decreases in the first year of contraction. Fourth, the real wage rate has no common feature. Finally, labor shares with and without "labor income of self-employment" imputed from self-employment income are almost parallel (except for Japan), and their movements are also similar, though they move differently for some years.

To explain these facts, I examine three types of model (or theory)—Kaldorian theory, real-business-cycle theory, and new Keynesian theory—but the focus is on Kaldor's approach—hence, the book's subtitle, *A Kaldorian Analysis*.

Kaldor's original model of income distribution, which he called the *Keynesian theory*, was the model of full employment (1955–1956). I discuss this model, including his background for model construction in relation to historical constancies. One of the strongest criticisms of his model is that it is incomplete in the underemployment economy. Some Keynesians complete the model by introducing the first postulate of the classical theory of employment, which was maintained by Keynes himself. I present two alternative Kaldorian models that are based on Kaldor's standpoint and do not include the marginal productivity principles. Unlike Kaldor's original model, these two alternative models are explicitly constructed in both nominal (money) and gross terms.

Model A, the employment-decision approach, and Model B, the markup pricing approach represent crucial assumptions and functions. Model B may be called a Kaleckian type. Model A is based on an assumption that employment is a positive function of investment. Labor productivity is also a positive function of employment that reflects the operating rate of capital and a kind of labor hoarding in the business cycle.

Under the limited conditions of my Kaldorian models (they are simple and in the short run), I show that the models have a fairly good interpretative value. The employment-decision-approach model, for example, has the potential for explaining most of my stylized facts.

Although this book is not a comprehensive study of real-business-cycle (RBC) theory and new Keynesian (NK) theory, I assess each from the viewpoint of my present purpose of research. Plosser's paper "Understanding Real Business Cycles" (1989) and Ball, Mankiw, and Romer's paper "The New Keynesian Economics and the Output-Inflation Trade-Off" (1988) are presented as representative of each of these theories, respectively. These models are less concerned about explaining stylized facts in the business cycle and have difficulty in explaining the change of variables in the labor market, particularly the relative share of labor and productivity.

My two alternative Kaldorian models are fairly effective in explaining the changes of macroeconomic variables in the business cycle. However, these models suggest a research agenda for future work—namely—determinants of investment, government policy and international trade, and the test of the models and model calibration.

Some questions remain regarding further development of these models, particularly the employment-decision model—testing the model, determining the treatment of the money wage rate (which I have treated as given), extending the model to the long run, and finally, if these investigations can be done successfully, fully developing arguments about policy relevance.

ACKNOWLEDGMENTS

I hope that this book will partially redeem the many debts, both intellectual and personal, I owe to others. From the beginning of my full-time research at the University of Buckingham until now, I owe a great deal to the former chairman of Business Studies, Jim Rafferty. I first met Jim in the summer of 1988 at St. Andrew's University, Osaka, where I was professor of economics. At that time we discussed research issues in my capacity as head of St. Andrew's Research Institute. Following a return visit by Jim to Japan in 1991, St. Andrew's University and the University of Buckingham formalized a sister university relationship.

An important feature of this relationship was the reciprocal access offered by the universities to members of staff to conduct research. For many years I had harbored the desire to complete a doctorate at a British University, and I expressed this wish to Jim, who kindly made arrangements for me to come to Buckingham. My own university also took a positive view about my wishes and kindly provided me with the opportunity to take extended study leave to carry out my research.

Since my arrival at Buckingham, Jim has been very helpful in discussing my research as my Buckingham supervisor. He also has supported me in obtaining the practical vital necessities of undertaking research by arranging computer access and library use and introducing me to other researchers. He has listened to my ideas in their formative stages, commented on and checked my draft chapters, and given me various suggestions along the way.

Professor Kent Matthews at Liverpool John Moores University guided me with my thesis as my external supervisor, providing a great deal of stimulus and many helpful suggestions about the structure and content of my research. My discussions with Kent have been very rewarding and a consistent source of encouragement.

Professor Martin Ricketts (dean of the School of Accounting, Business and Economics at the University of Buckingham) has shown interest in my work and kindly assisted with arrangements in cooperation with Jim, introducing Kent as my external supervisor. Martin has not only given me helpful suggestions but has facilitated my research by introducing me to the Cranfield Management Information Resource Centre and helping me to obtain some other necessary resources. He also kindly read my draft of Chapter 2, making valuable suggestions in the process.

Professor Robert Daniel kindly helped with the mathematical verification, particularly when I had a mathematical problem in December 1993. I was also given some useful suggestions by Professor Anthony Atkinson during our discussions at the London School of Economics in January 1994.

This book has been germinating in my mind and other writings for over twenty years. Throughout this time many of the discussions I have had with my early teachers contributed to my ideas about macroeconomic variables.

Professor Emeritus Takasuke Suenaga at both Osaka City University and Kobe University of Commerce was my supervisor while I was a postgraduate student between 1967 and 1971 at Osaka City University. Professor Suenaga guided me with my studies, suggesting Kalecki's works and the work of Keynesians such as Joan Robinson, Nicholas Kaldor, and Roy Harrod as suitable areas for intellectual inquiry. I had primarily studied Marxian theory as an undergraduate, and in those days in Japan, Professor Suenaga was one of the most prominent researchers who covered both Marxian and modern theories. Professor Suenaga kindly paid attention to my teaching and work for many years. As recently as this year I received encouragement from him reminding me that it is never too late and the most important thing is to possess a sincere attitude toward the science as a student. For his support over many years, I am extremely grateful.

The other supervisor in my postgraduate days was the late Professor Yoshizo Yoshida at Osaka City University, who was a specialist in business-cycle theory and economic policy. When we discussed theoretical matters, he often reminded me of the social relevance of theory, and I gained much from attending his seminars for about three years after leaving the university.

I was a visiting fellow at the University of Lancaster from 1982 to 1983 and in the summer of 1984. During this time I was engaged in estimating U.K. income distribution under the supervision of John King, who is currently working for La Trobe University in Australia. At that time Professor Jim Taylor also assisted me in some computer analysis, and I am grateful to them both.

I owe much to a large number of other persons at both Buckingham and

St. Andrew's universities. I am grateful to the chairman of Business Studies, Douglas Stoddart, for facilitating my research and heartily paying attention to my progress, to Malcolm Rees for giving me the use of his computer, to John Galletly for computer suggestions, and to other faculty members in the School of ABE. I am particularly grateful to my colleagues in Business Studies. A former university computer technician, Devin Deng, provided various kinds of practical computer application analysis, and secretaries Doreen Munn, Janice Circuit, and Linda Waterman, and librarians Richard and Swee Har Newell and Margaret Charles, all provided valuable assistance.

I would like to express my gratitude to the former dean of the Faculty of Economics at St. Andrew's University, Naoto Yamashita, who unfortunately passed away suddenly in May 1994. When he was dean, he kindly accepted my request to undertake research at Buckingham and extended my stay in England when this was necessary. I would also like to thank the current dean, Professor Akimasa Katsura, for obtaining the necessary resources and assistance of the Computer Centre staff and librarians of St. Andrew's University.

Finally, I should like to offer my special thanks to my family—my wife, Masako, and my son, Muneyoshi. They patiently allowed me to live a separate life while engaged in my research in England. In addition, Masako searched painstakingly for large amounts of material in my office and den, and sometimes at the University Library, despatching them with careful attention. And I would like to express my gratitude to Akiko, my mother-in-law, for her welcomed letters and the encouragement I gained from them.

ABBREVIATIONS

ABBREVIATIONS

ANA	*Annual Report on National Accounts*
ARC	Annual Rate of Change
BMR	Ball, Mankiw, and Romer
CPI	Consumer Price Index
CSP	*Capital Stock of Private Enterprises*
EE	employees in employment
EG	*Employment Gazette*
ERP	*Economic Report of the President*
ET	*Economic Trends*
ETAS	*Economic Trends: Annual Supplement*
FE	firm employees
GCS	gross capital stock
GCSR	gross capital stock ratio of unincorporated to incorporated enterprises
GDP	gross domestic product
GDPC	gross domestic product at constant prices
GDPM	gross domestic product at market prices
GNP	gross national product
GNPC	gross national product at constant prices
GNPM	gross national product at market prices
GTP	gross trading profits

GTS	gross trading surplus
IE	income from employment
IS	income from self-employment
JPD	Japan datastream
LIS	labor income from self-employment
NA	*(United Kingdom) National Accounts*
NAE	*National Account and Expenditure*
NCS	net capital stock
NCSR	net capital stock ratio of unincorporated to incorporated enterprises
NFE	nonfirm employees
NI	national income
NOP	net operating profits
OPE	output per person employed
OPI	operating profits of incorporated enterprises
PBS	private business sector
PBT	profits before income taxes
PI	profits of incorporated enterprises
RAF	resident armed forces
RBC	real business cycle
RH	*Rodo Hakusho [White Paper on Labor]*
RPI	retail price index
SCB	*Survey of Current Business*
SE	stockholder's equity
UKD	United Kingdom datastream
ULC	unit labor costs
USD	United States datastream
WE	workforce in employment

SYMBOLS

Symbols (English)

C	investment-output ratio, I/Y
D	depreciation
e	price level
I	investment
I^*	investment sustaining the present number of labor employed
I_r	investment in real terms
i_r	per capita investment in real terms, I_r/L
K	capital stock
k	capital intensity, K/L
K_v	value of capital stock
L	labor force employed
L^*	labor force employed in the case of $I = I^*$

L_{fk}	labor force employed under full employment of capital
L_{fl}	labor force employed under fully employed labor
m	"degree of monopoly" rate
P	profits
r	markup rate
r'	"risk premium" rate
S	savings (total)
S_p	savings of profits
s_p	propensity to save from profits
S_w	savings of wages (and salaries)
s_w	propensity to save from wages (and salaries)
v	capital-output ratio
W	wages (and salaries)
w	real wage rate (in Kaldor's original model of Chapter 3)
w'	minimum real wage rate
Y	output
y	per capita output, Y/L

Symbols (Greek)

δ	rate of depreciation of capital
μ	labor productivity per head
π	profit rate
ρ_c	relative share of profits (property)
ρ_l	relative share of labor
ω	real wage rate
ω_m	money wage rate

Symbols for the New Keynesian Theory of Chapter 5

F	fixed cost of adjustment
g	growth rate
g_t	trend growth of g per unit of time
p	aggregate price level
p_i	firm i's price
p_i^*	firm i's profit-maximizing price
t	unit of time
$W(t)$	Weiner process (random walk innovations)
x	nominal aggregate demand
y	aggregate spending
$\bar{y}$	natural rate of output growth at rate μ, $\bar{y} = \mu$
θ_i	firm i's specific shock
λ	price change intervals of length
λ_i	firm i's price change interval of length
λ^E	Nash equilibrium for λ

ν	elasticity of firm i's profit-maximizing real price with respect to y
$\bar{\pi}$	average inflation rate
σ_θ	standard deviation of firm-specific shocks
σ_θ^2	variance of firm-specific shocks
σ_x	standard deviation of demand
σ_x^2	variance of demand shock
τ	coefficient of the change in nominal demand

PROFITS, WAGES, AND PRODUCTIVITY IN THE BUSINESS CYCLE

1. INTRODUCTION

Since Ricardo, one of the principal questions facing economists has been how to present a theory of income distribution. Ricardo (1817, p. 5) remarks on the historical fact that "in different stages of society, the proportions of the whole produce of the earth which will be allotted to each of these classes [the proprietor of the land, the owner of the stock or capital, and the laborers], under the name of rent, profit and wages will be essentially different." He continues this theme by pointing out that "To determine the laws which regulate this distribution is the principal problem in political economy."

Kaldor (1955–1956) shares with Ricardo an appreciation for the importance of income distribution. However, his emphasis is that the theory of income distribution should explain a relative stability of the distributive shares. Kaldor presented a bird's-eye view of the main strands of nineteenth- and twentieth-century economic thought—namely, Ricardian or classical theory, Marxian, neoclassical or marginalist theory, and Keynesian. He proposed his idea as the *Keynesian theory*, which now is called *Kaldor's model of income distribution.*

There are two basic strands of thought in modern income distribution theory. One is the Keynesian model based on the theory of the multiplier and the idea of widow's cruse.[1] The other is the neoclassical. There has been heated polemic between these schools of thought, especially in the 1960s, with each asserting the value of its interpretation. Then a synthesis approach appeared. Economic terms such as *investment, savings*, and the *relative share of labor* are macroeconomic totals, but they have a relationship to microeconomic theory.

In this respect, some economists attempted to construct a model based partly on microeconomic theory. This approach may be referred as a *synthesis* or *general* theory of income distribution.[2]

This book addresses changes in macroeconomic variables in the business cycle, such as the labor share, the profit rate, labor productivity, and the real wage rate. First I try to establish the facts about these changes in three countries—the United Kingdom, the United States, and Japan—and then attempt to explain these facts. For this purpose, I examine three models—Kaldor's theory, the real business cycle theory, and the new Keynesian theory. Throughout the focus is on Kaldor's approach—hence, the book's subtitle, *A Kaldorian Analysis.*

Kaldor's first model appeared almost half a century ago (1955–1956). That model was simple, but the historical constancies that he recognized began to seem doubtful.[3]

This book carefully examines Kaldor's model of income distribution and interprets it by reformulating the model, making clear what the model will explain and what its weaknesses are. Kaldor's model has interpretative value in a full-employment economy. He constructed his model assuming full employment and stated that, when his restraint conditions to the model are satisfied, "there will be an inherent tendency to growth and an inherent tendency to full employment" (1955–1956, p. 235).

Advanced capitalist societies are not stable, however, and suffer from business fluctuations. If we want to explain how economic variables change during the business cycle, we have to deal with an underemployment economy. In this respect, Kaldor's model has a theoretical weakness. His model, therefore, is incomplete in the underemployment economy (refer to Chapter 3). To complete the model, some Keynesians introduced the first postulate of the classical theory of employment—namely, "the wage is equal to the marginal product of labour" (Keynes, 1936, p. 5).[4] As was mentioned earlier, this is a *general* or *synthesis* model of income distribution. This is the product of a compromise between the Keynesian hypothesis that investment is an independent variable and the marginal productivity principles. Rather than express it in this way, I present two alternative Kaldorian models from a different viewpoint that are based on Kaldor's standpoint and do not include the marginal productivity principles.[5] Unlike Kaldor's original model, the alternative models in this book are explicitly constructed in both nominal (money) terms and gross terms.[6]

It might be useful to mention here some important points in relation to the conclusions reached in Chapter 6. Each model discussed here has its usefulness and weaknesses. However, for the purpose of explaining the changes of macroeconomic variables in the business cycle, Kaldorian models are fairly effective. Among others, the employment decision approach (Model A) presented in Chapter 4 has possibilities for explaining most of our stylized facts. However, this model has two weaknesses in terms of presenting a more elaborate explanation—namely, it is too simple and deals only with the short run. Questions remain about the further development of this model, especially in testing the model and determining how it treats the money wage rate.

The plan of this book is as follows. First, the facts of macroeconomic variables in relation to the business cycle are provided in Chapter 2, and Kaldor's model of income distribution is presented in Chapter 3. Chapter 4 provides two types of Kaldorian models of the underemployment economy and examines their interpretative values. In Chapter 5, the real business cycle theory and the new Keynesian theory are explained, and their interpretative value is argued. Finally, Chapter 6 concludes with a summary, and questions raised by the nature of this inquiry are explored as areas for future empirical and theoretical investigation.

NOTES

1. The widow's cruse is an allegorical expression regarding the determinants of profits. Refer to note 1 of Chapter 3 for details.

2. Sen (1963, p. 57) calls this the "General Theory" model of Keynesian income distribution. The same understanding is seen in Weintraub (1958), Atsumi (1960), Okamoto (1967), Yasui (1969), and others. Refer to note 1 of Chapter 4 for Sen's argument.

3. See "Historical Constancies" in Chapter 3 for an argument relating to this matter.

4. Keynes himself maintains this first postulate as heretofore subject only to the same qualifications as in classical theory. This means that, "with a given organization, equipment and technique, real wages and the volume of output (and hence of employment) are uniquely correlated, so that, in general, then an increase in employment can only occur to the accompaniment of a decline in the rate of real wages" (1936, p. 17). Regarding my argument on this point, particularly in an underemployment economy, see "A Symmetrical Change in Productivity Growth" in Chapter 2 and assumption v and an explanation of equation (5) in Chapter 4.

5. Refer to note 11 in Chapter 3 for Kaldor's argument on the marginal productivity principles.

6. We consider these two kinds of treatment are a fairly important. For an argument on nominal terms and gross terms, see notes 6 and 5 in Chapter 3, respectively. The reasons for these treatment are stated in Chapter 4.

2. SOME FACTS ABOUT THE TYPICAL BUSINESS CYCLE

This chapter attempts to answer the following questions about the United Kingdom, the United States, and Japan: What kind of changes occur in macroeconomic variables—such as the labor share, the profit rate, labor productivity, and the real wage rate—throughout the business cycle, and can any regularities be found in these changes? The observation period covers at least three business cycles from 1970 to 1992.

This chapter first presents the overall results of this study and then explains the framework used in establishing the facts and the data source for calculation. Estimates for each country are provided in detail, and a few factors that condition the observed facts are examined. Finally, the stylized facts are summarized and explained.

SOME FACTS IN GENERAL

In this section, some observed facts are discussed in the following order: labor share, profit rate, labor productivity, and the real wage rate. Then observations are made about the relationship between estimates with and without an imputed labor income from self-employment (LIS).

First, no common feature is observed in labor-share movements among the three countries compared. Countercyclical movements of the labor share are most clear in Japan, the United Kingdom displays some ambiguity during the observation period, and the United States is most ambiguous. However, a feature common to these three countries is that in general the labor share increases in the first year of contraction and decreases in the first year of expansion, though there are some exceptions.

Second, as might be generally expected, the profit rate moves procyclically to the business cycle. This feature is more or less common among the three countries compared. However, the cyclical change of the profit rate does not always coincide with trough or peak years in the business cycle.

The third fact concerns productivity growth, which shows strong cyclical movements. In particular, a symmetrical change in productivity growth in the phase of the business cycle is observed in the three countries: productivity (the labor productivity per person employed) sharply increases in the first year of expansion in terms of the growth rate and decreases in the first year of contraction. The phenomenon is also supported by the change of unit labor costs.

The fourth fact relates to the real wage rate. Here there is no common feature between the countries. In the United States, the growth of the real wage rate becomes negative in the first year of contraction but becomes positive in the first year of expansion. A similar change for the employees' case (calculated by *IE*/*EE*) (see the following section for the equations) in Japan is observed in the 1970s (with an exception of 1977).

The cycles (the procyclical change) in the real wage rate are most clear in the case of the United States, followed by Japan for the employees' case in the 1970s. The growth of the real wage rate in Japan has stabilized since 1981. In the United Kingdom, the change of the real wage rate has no regularity; however, it tends to decrease relatively in the first year of expansion and also in the first year of contraction.

Finally, we observe the relationship between the estimates with and without LIS imputed from self-employment income. The labor shares with and without LIS are almost parallel (except for Japan), and their movements are also similar, though they move differently for some years. These features hold true for the three countries and also for the real wage rate.

However, each country has its particular feature, reflecting on its structural change or specific business situation in the economy. The gap between two kinds of estimate in the United Kingdom widened in the 1980s, especially in the latter half of the decade. In the United States, this gap became fairly narrow during the period 1980 to 1983. The gap in Japan has narrowed continuously since 1977.

COMPARATIVE METHODS

Equations for Calculation

The following points are considered in creating equations for calculation. First, the focus is not on a particular industry or sector but on the whole economy and the dynamic change of the macroeconomic variables in the business cycle. Second, as far as possible, the same framework is used to compare the three countries. When common data are lacking, however, the second-best framework is used, or supplementary data are substituted.

The Labor Share

Two kinds of labor share are estimated. The first kind is calculated by

$$\frac{\text{Income from employment (IE)}}{\text{GDP at market prices (GDPM)}} \text{ and } \frac{\text{IE}}{\text{GNPM}}.$$

When we aim to estimate the relative share of labor in a whole economy, we have to impute the income from self-employment (IS) between wages and profits since self-employment income is a mixture of profits and wages. The two basic methods of imputation are the *labor* and *asset bases*.[1]

Here a rather simple method of imputation is based on the asset basis, supposing that capital of the unincorporated enterprises gains the same profit rate as that of incorporated enterprises. The labor basis requires more complicated assumptions than the asset basis of each country.[2] Then we have an equation with LIS of the second kind:

$$\frac{\text{IE + Labor income from self-employment (LIS)}}{\text{GNPM}},$$

where LIS is imputed by using an asset basis.[3]

The Profit Rate

The profit rate is calculated by the following (for the United Kingdom some other profit rate indexes are additionally quoted from *Datastream*):

$$\text{United Kingdom: } \frac{\text{Gross trading profits (GTP)}}{\text{Net capital stock (NCS) of companies}}, \text{ and}$$

$$\frac{\text{GTP + Gross trading surplus (GTS)}}{\text{Net capital stock (NCS) of companies and public corporations}}.$$

$$\text{United States: } \frac{\text{Profits before income taxes (PBT)}}{\text{Stockholders' equity}}, \text{ and}$$

$$\frac{\text{Profits of incorporated enterprises (PI, Net)}}{\text{Net capital stock of incorporated enterprises}}.$$

$$\text{Japan: } \frac{\text{PI (Net)}}{\text{Gross capital stock (GCS) of incorporated enterprises}}, \text{ and}$$

$$\frac{\text{Operating profits of incorporated enterprises (OPI)}}{\text{GCS of incorporated enterprises}},$$

These equations are not exactly the same. For the United Kingdom, the denominator is taken in net terms, but the numerator is in gross terms. The profit rate by the equation is somewhat greater than the actual profit rate. For Japan, the denominator is in gross terms and at 1985 replacement cost, but the numerator is in net terms. In contrast with the United Kingdom, the calculated rate of profits is lower than the actual one. This is partly due to availability of data, in particular capital stock for Japan. However, despite of these differences, it is possible to observe the trend or the change of the profit rate in the business cycle.

Labor Productivity

Labor productivity is calculated by

$$\frac{\text{GDP at constant prices (GDPC)}}{\text{Workforce in employment (WE)}}, \text{ and/or } \frac{\text{GNPC}}{\text{WE}}.$$

Some supplementary calculation is done for the whole economy or for some industries.[4]

The change of unit labor costs by whole economy, sector or industry is additionally calculated using the index of the unit labor costs.

The Real Wage Rate

The real wage rate is obtained by

Annual Rate of Change (ARC) of (IE/Employees) – ARC of Consumer Price Index (CPI) or Retail Price Index (RPI) and ARC of {(IE + LIS)/WE} – ARC of CPI (or RPI).

Data

Data Source

Data[5] are mostly from *Datastream* as of October 25, and November 1, 1993, supplied by the respective government institutions.

First of all, annual rather than quarterly data are used because an annual base seems to be most suitable for seeing fundamental changes; quarterly data are more affected by noise elements. Nonetheless, it might be necessary to use quarterly data for a finer analysis. In this case, a proper adjustment is necessary for the case lacking quarterly data. Second, adjusted trough and peak years are used to consider the whole economy. An explanation follows.

Trough and Peak Years Adjusted

We adjusted turning point years indicated by the cyclical indicator (coincident, yearly) for the real growth rate of GDP (and GNP).[6] So some trough and

Figure 2.1. Cyclical Indicators or Diffusion Index, United Kingdom, United States, Japan, 1970 to 1992 (coincident, yearly)

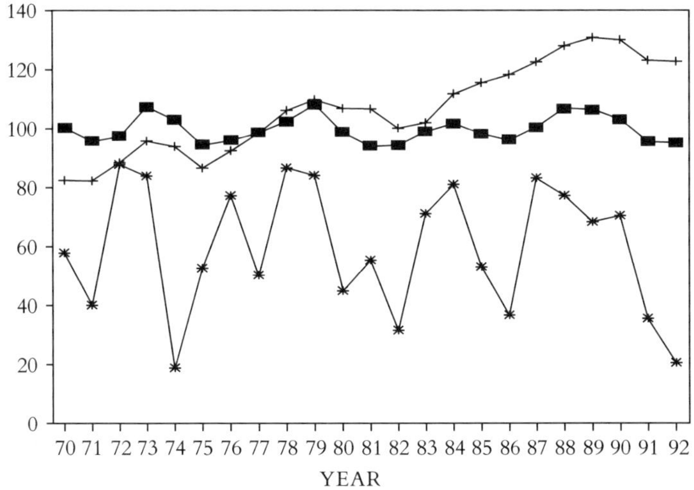

■ = United Kingdom cyclical indicator
+ = United States cyclical indicator
✱ = Japan diffusion index

Table 2.1. Trough and Peak Years After Adjustments for the United Kingdom, United States, and Japan, 1970 to 1992

	Trough	Peak
United Kingdom	1972 (trough, 1971)[a]	1973
	1975	1979
	1981	1983 (peak, 1984)[a]
	1984 (trough, 1985)[a]	1988
	1992	
United States		1973
	1975	1979
	1982	1988 (peak, 1989)[a]
	1991 (trough, 1992)[a]	
Japan	1971	1973
	1974	1976
	1977	1979
	1983 (trough, 1982)[a]	1985
	1986	1991

a. The trough and peak year are different from that of the cyclical indicator. The year before adjustment is shown in parentheses.

peak years are different from those of the cyclical indicator. Figure 2.1 shows cyclical indicators for the United Kingdom and the United States, and a diffusion index for Japan.

Respective trough and peak years after adjustments are shown in Table 2.1.[7]

RESULTS IN DETAIL

The Labor Share

United Kingdom

Observing the U.K. labor share as shown in Figures 2.2a and 2.2b,[8] it will be seen that trough and peak years of the business cycle do not always coincide with peak and trough years of the labor share in the business cycle, but the labor share, as a whole, moves countercyclically. The labor share movement is observed as a downward or upward trend. However, focusing on trough and peak years in the business cycle, the labor share in both with LIS and IE/GNP cases is seen to move countercyclically in the 1970s (with an exception of 1973) but to show no regular movement since 1980. A symmetrical change in the labor share is observed during the business cycle: it increases in the first year of contraction and decreases in the first year of expansion (with the exception of 1973 and of one estimate for 1984).[9] The labor share movements of both with and without imputed LIS are almost parallel in the United Kingdom.

United States

In Figures 2.3a and 2.3b, the U.S. labor share in general does not seem to have any regularity. Focusing on trough and peak years in the business cycle, it seems that for the estimate with LIS the movements are procyclical in the 1970s and rather countercyclical since 1980 (with an exception of 1982). For the IE/GDP case movements are countercyclical during the observation period except for 1982 but are more irregular in the IE/GNP case. A symmetrical change in the labor share between the first years of expansion and contraction is more or less established (with the exception of 1989 and of one estimate for 1976 and one for 1992). The pattern is the same in the United Kingdom. The labor share movements of both with and without imputed LIS are almost parallel, although there are slight variations in one or two years.

Japan

As shown in Figures 2.4a and 2.4b, the countercyclical movement of the labor share is most clear in Japan. Trough and peak years of the business cycle correspond to the respective peak and trough years in the change of the labor share (with the exception of the years 1976 and 1991, and of one estimate for 1973).[10] Concerning a symmetrical change in the labor share between the first years of expansion and contraction above mentioned, there are two exceptions of 1973 and 1975 for the employees' case; however, for the case with LIS there are more distortions (exceptions) in the 1970s.[11] The labor share gap between with and without imputation of income from self-employment is seen to be narrowing; however, the countercyclical movements remain constant.

Figure 2.2a. Share of Labor in National Income (%), United Kingdom, 1970 to 1992

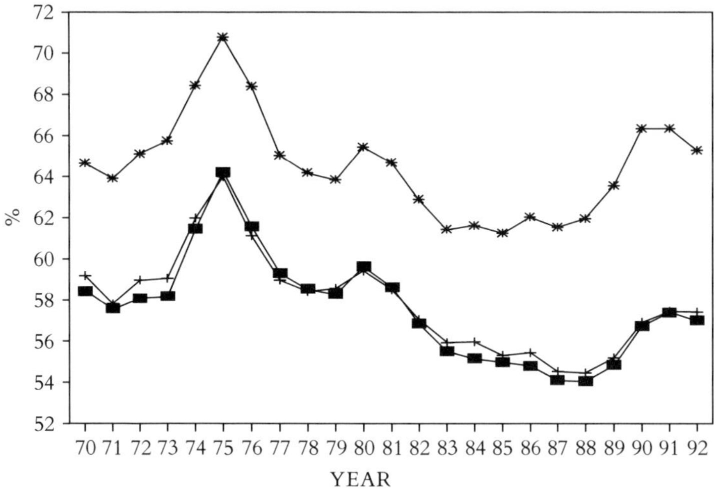

+ = IE/GDP (UKD8/UKD4)
■ = IE/GNP (UKD8/UKD3)
✳ = (IE + LIS)/GNP (UKD8 + LIS/UKD3)
LIS = IS − GTP*NCSR (Ratio of unincorporated to incorporated enterprises) (see Appendix 2B Data). UKD8 stands for U.K. *Datastream* number in Appendix 2B.

Figure 2.2b. Change in Labor's Share of National Income (%), United Kingdom, 1971 to 1992

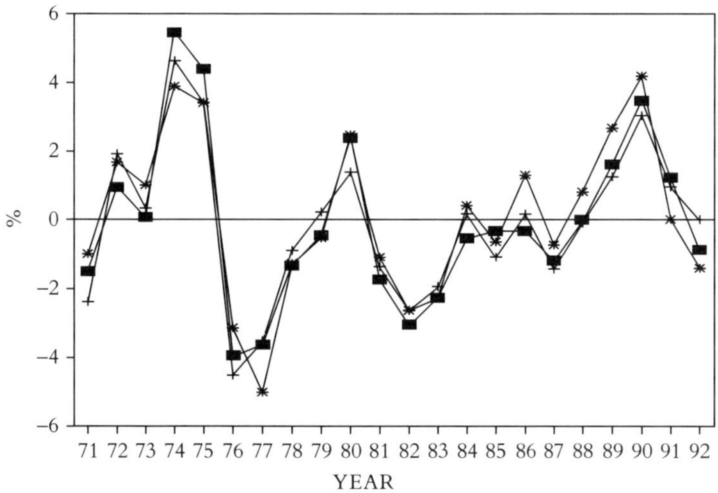

Note: Symbols are the same as in Figure 2.2a.

Figure 2.3a. Share of Labor in National Income (%), United States, 1970 to 1992

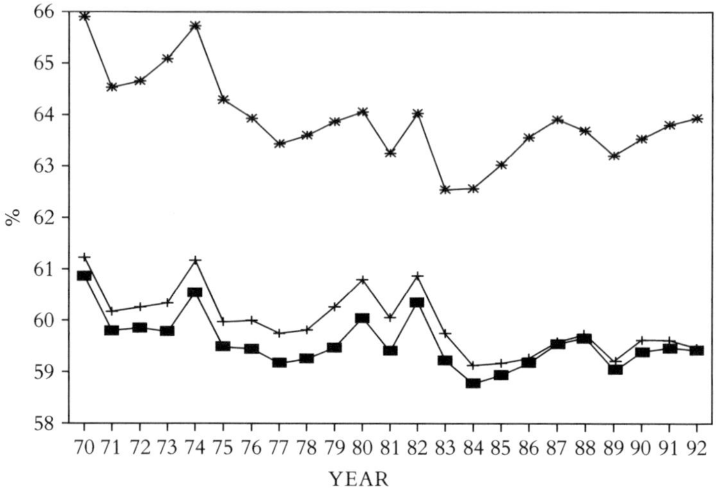

+ = IE/GDP (USD12/USD5)
■ = IE/GNP (USD12/USD1)
✱ = (IE + LIS)/GNP,
where LIS = IS (Farm and nonfarm) – PI*NCSR = (USD15 + USD16) – USD17* (T6 SCB).
USD12 stands for U.S. *Datastream* number in Appendix 2B.

Figure 2.3b. Change in Labor's Share of National Income (%), United States, 1971 to 1992

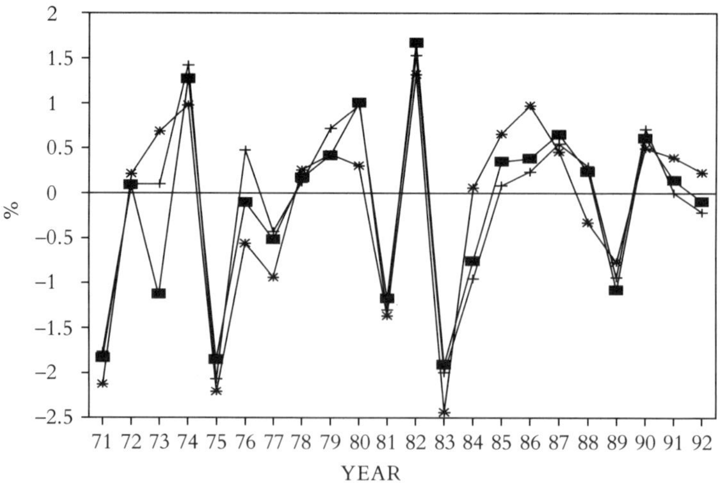

Note: Symbols are the same as in Figure 2.3a above.

Figure 2.4a. Share of Labor in National Income (%), Japan, 1970 to 1991

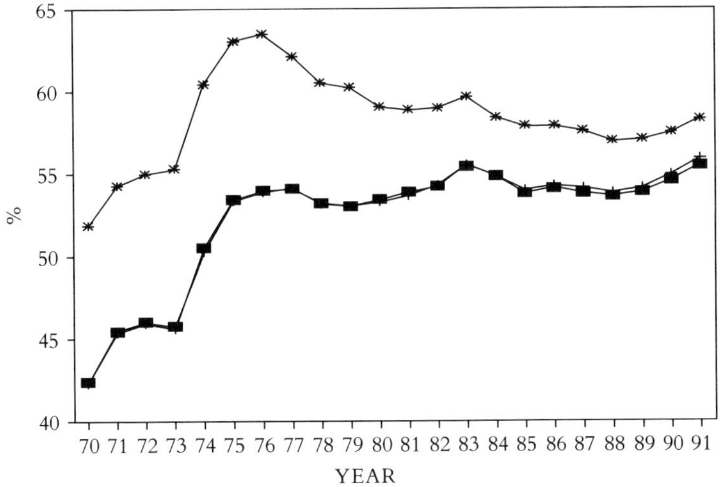

+ = IE/GDP (JPD5/(Part 1[2]IV, 1 *ANA*))
■ = IE/GNP (JPD5/JPD1)
✱ = (IE + LIS)/GNP,
where LIS = IS − PI*GCSR
= (Part 1[2]IV, 2 *ANA*; T1 *CSP*).
JPD5 stands for Japan *Datastream* number in Appendix 2B.

Figure 2.4b. Change in Labor's Share of National Income (%), Japan, 1971 to 1991

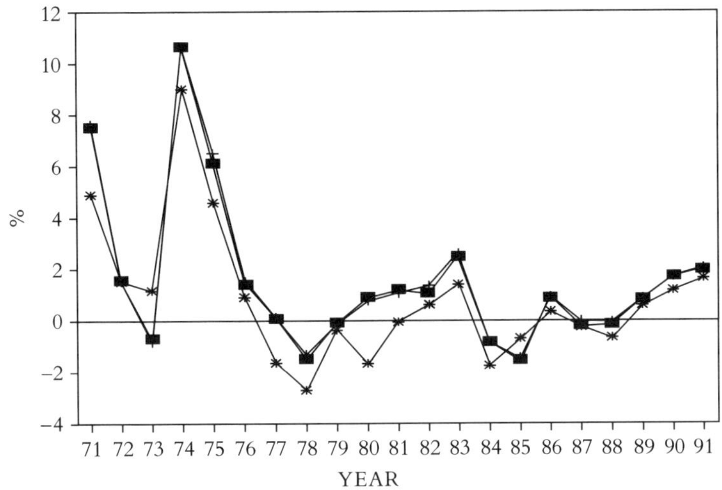

Note: Symbols are the same as in Figure 2.4a above.

A large increase of the labor share in the first half of the 1970s relates to the following two facts. During these periods, the Japanese economy underwent a drastic structural change triggered by rapidly increasing oil prices.[12] The era of high Japanese economic growth ended with the first oil shock, which marked a turning point, and the Japanese economy moved onto a more modest growth path (5 to 6 percent).[13] The labor share continued to increase in the first half of the 1970s.

The Profit Rate

United Kingdom

In Figures 2.5a and 2.5b, the profit rates in the United Kingdom are seen to move more or less pro-cyclically with the business cycle (with some exceptions for the early 1970s). Further consideration of the early 1970s would be necessary to take account of the effects of worldwide inflation. There might be a possibility of under- or overestimation of profits under such a high rate of inflation.[14]

Owing to the lack of proper data, the denominator of Figures 2.5a is taken in net terms. The difference of the profit rate between manufacturing and whole industries is not in question here; however, the profit rate in manufacturing is far lower than for industry as a whole, especially during the period from the end of the 1970s to the end of the 1980s.[15] This is shown in Figure 2.5b.

United States

Observing the U.S. profit rates for manufacturing corporations and all private corporations in Figure 2.6, it will be seen that they move cyclically. The trough and peak of the profit rate fluctuations do not always coincide with the trough and peak years of the business cycle.

Japan

Figure 2.7 (incorporated enterprises) shows that the net operating profit rate moves procyclically. The net profit rate on the national account base also moves procyclically but shows a different movement for the years 1977 and 1989 to 1991.[16]

Labor Productivity

United Kingdom

Labor productivity in the United Kingdom shows a symmetrical change in the process of the business cycle (see Figure 2.8a). Productivity sharply increases in the first year of expansion and sharply decreases in the first year

Figure 2.5a. Rate of Profits (%), United Kingdom, 1970 to 1992

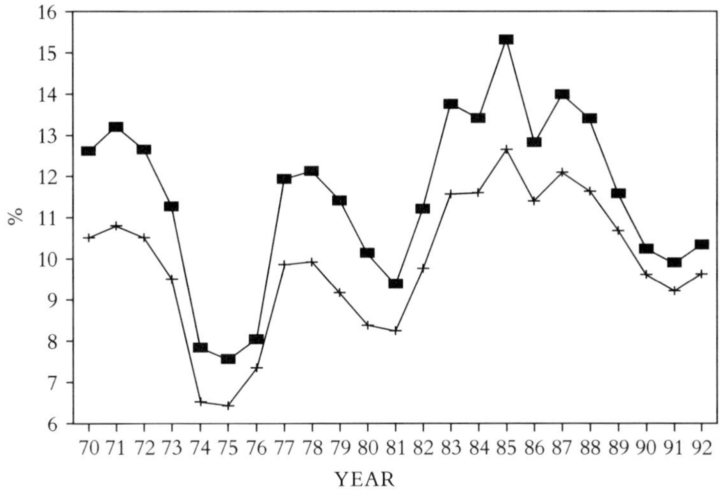

■ = GTP/NCS (Companies)
+ = (GTP + GTS)/NCS (Companies + Public corporations)
See Appendix 2B.

Figure 2.5b. Rate of Profits (%), United Kingdom, 1970 to 1992

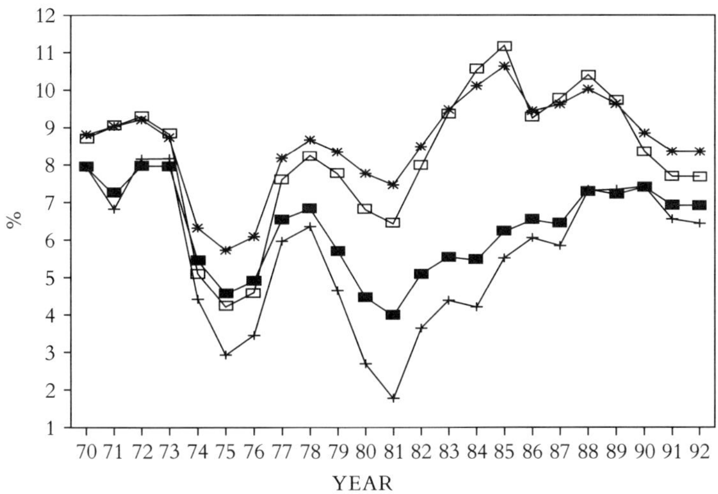

□ = Net profit rate (all industries and commercial companies) (UKD10)
✱ = Gross profit rate (same as above) (UKD9)
■ = Gross profit rate (manufacturing) (UKD11)
+ = Net profit rate (manufacturing) (UKD12)

Figure 2.6. Rate of Profits (%), United States, 1970 to 1992

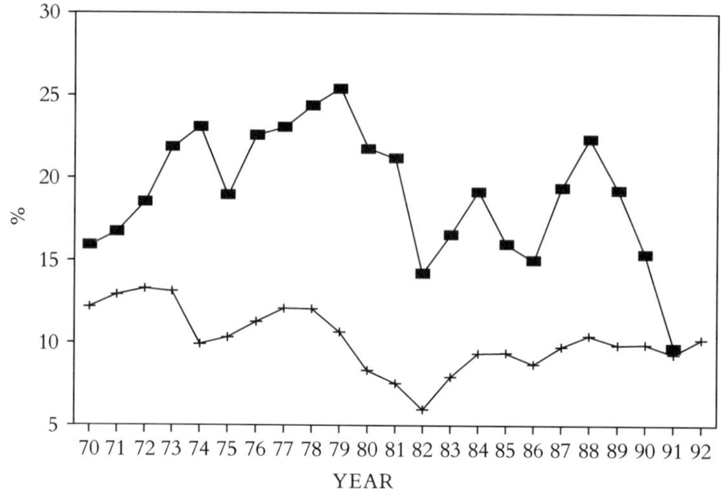

+ = PI/NCS (corporate) (USD17/(T6 *SCB*))
■ = PBT/SE (manufacturing) (T88 *ERP*)
See Appendix 2B for an adjustment for PBT/SE estimate.

Figure 2.7. Rate of Profits (%), Japan, 1970 to 1992

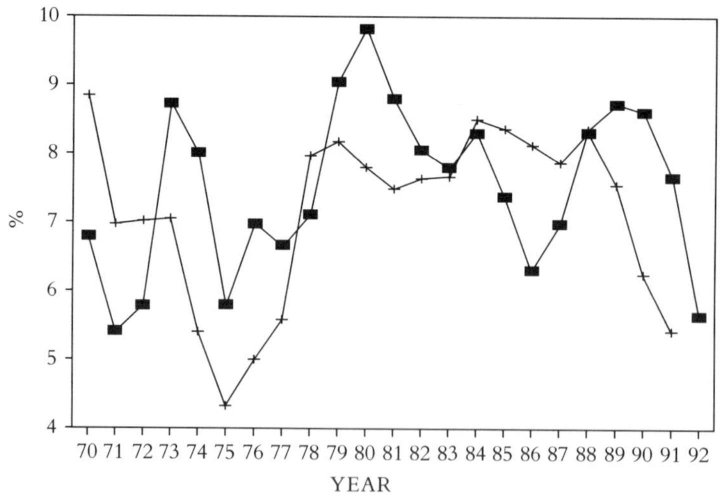

+ = PI/GCS (incorporated enterprises)
■ = NOP/GCS (incorporated enterprises)
See Appendix 2B.

of contraction, demonstrating negative growth in most cases as a whole economy. This symmetrical change is also indirectly confirmed by the change of unit labor costs (Figure 2.8b). The change of unit labor costs in manufacturing industry in the 1980s seems a puzzling phenomenon (especially for the years 1984 and 1989). This needs consideration in relation to the characteristic movement of the industry and also to its weight in the whole economy. It is simply caused by the fact that the cyclical trough and peak years in the manufacturing industry occurred not in 1984 and 1988 but in 1986 and 1989, respectively.[17]

United States

In Figure 2.9a, the same kind of symmetrical change as in the United Kingdom is seen. The symmetry in the United States is clearer than in the United Kingdom. The change in the unit labor costs provides a supplementary explanation (Figure 2.9b). The symmetrical change of the unit labor costs between the first years of contraction and expansion is also observed in both the private business sector and the manufacturing industry in the United States, but this is in a relative sense. It does not show negative growth very often during the observation period.

Japan

A similar symmetrical change to those of the United Kingdom and the United States is observed in Japan (Figure 2.10a). A different movement is observed in all industries in 1975. This would seem to be related to the fact that the trough year of manufacturing and indeed all industries was in 1975. Figure 2.10b shows the change of the unit labor costs in manufacturing industry, and the same kind of symmetrical change as in both the United Kingdom and the United States is observed. Taking into consideration that the manufacturing trough year was 1975, the high rate of increase in 1975 for the unit labor costs is understandable.

The Real Wage Rate

United Kingdom

The change of the real wage rate has no regularity in the United Kingdom (Figure 2.11). It is likely to decrease in the growth rate both in the first years of expansion (except for 1985)[18] and of contraction (except for 1980).

United States

The real wage rate in the United States moves rather cyclically with some exceptional years (Figure 2.12), decreasing in the first year of contraction (negative growth) and increasing in the first year of expansion.

Figure 2.8a. Change in Labor Productivity (%), United Kingdom, 1971 to 1992

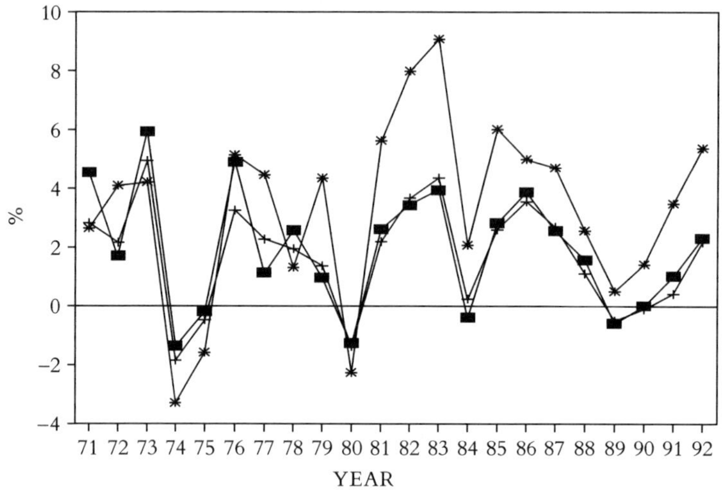

■ = GDP/WE; GDPD (Deflator) (UKD4/UKD5; UKD6)
✱ = Output per person employed (production industries) (UKD2)
+ = Same as above (whole economy) (UKD1)

Figure 2.8b. Change in Unit Labor Costs (%), United Kingdom, 1971 to 1992

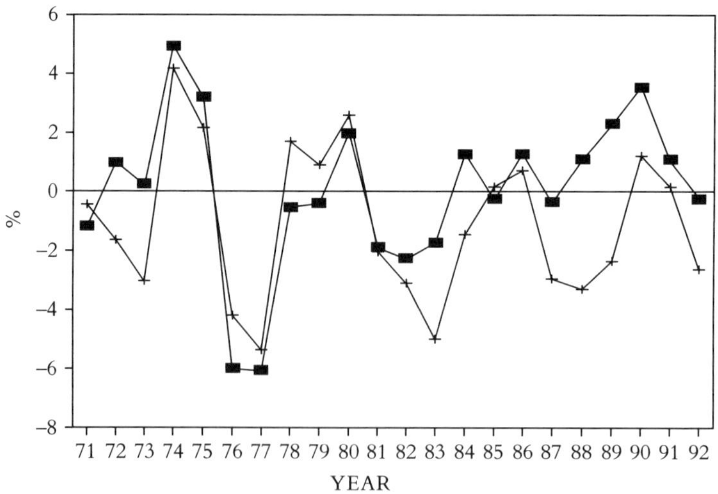

+ = ULC (manufacturing); GDPD (T24 *ETAS*, T5.8 *EG*; UKD6)
■ = ULC (whole economy); GDPD (same as above)
Both ULCs are deflated by the GDP deflator.

Figure 2.9a. Change in Labor Productivity (%), United States, 1971 to 1992

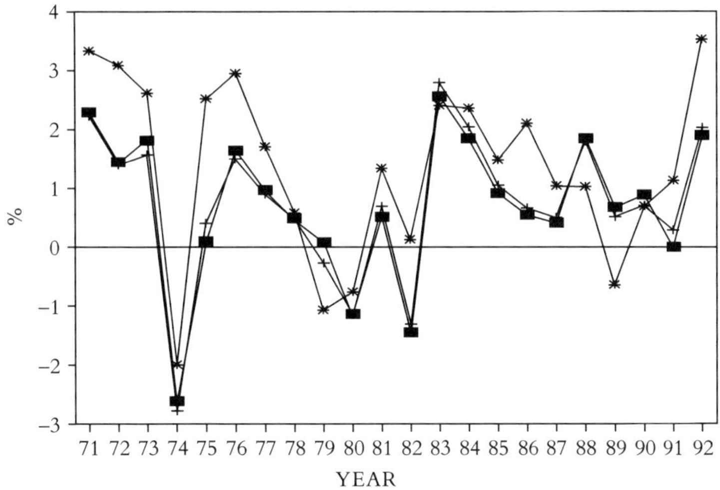

+ = GDP/WE; GDPD (USD5/USD7; USD6)
■ = GNP/WE; GNPD (USD1/USD7; USD4)
* = Output per hour of all persons (PBS = private business sector) (USD13)

Figure 2.9b. Change in Unit Labor Costs (%), United States, 1971 to 1992

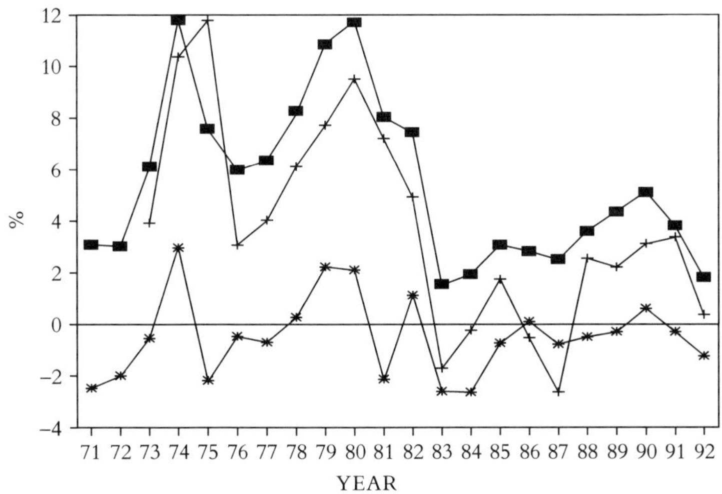

+ = ULC (manufacturing) (USD19)
■ = ULC (PBS) (USD22)
* = ULC (PBS)*; deflated by GNP deflator (USD22, USD6)

Figure 2.10a. Change in Labor Productivity (%), Japan, 1971 to 1992

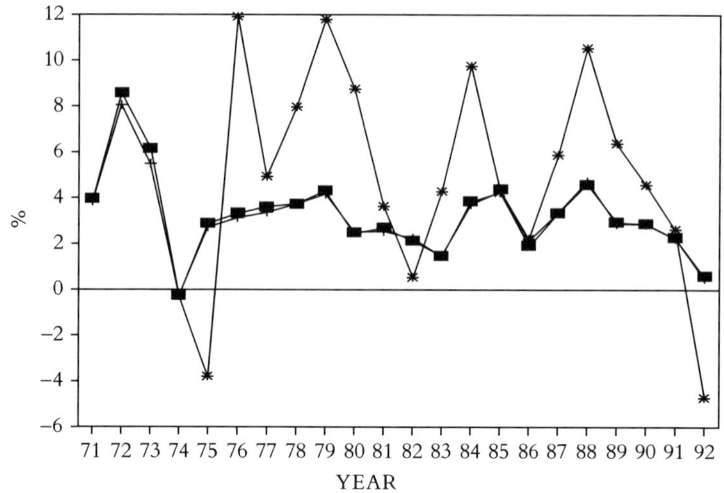

+ = GDP (at constant price)/WE (JPD11/JPD3)
■ = GNP/WE; GNPD (JPD1/JPD3; JPD2)
✱ = Labor Productivity Index (all industries) (JPD8)

Figure 2.10b. Change in Unit Labor Costs (%), Japan, 1974 to 1992

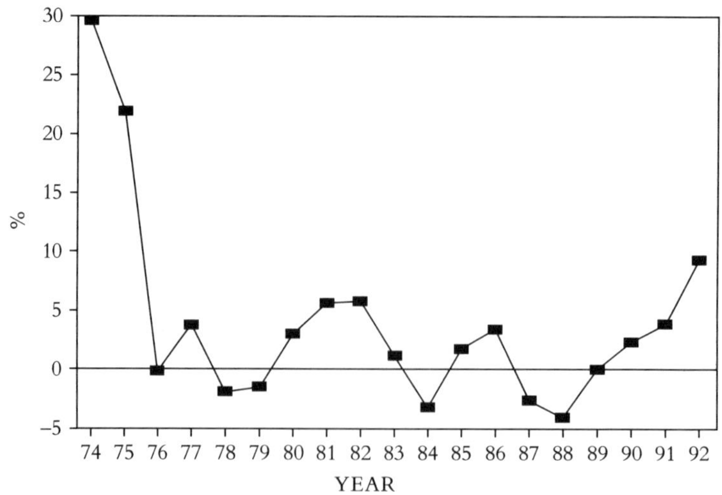

■ = ULC (manufacturing) (JPD7)

Figure 2.11. Change in the Real Wage Rate (%), United Kingdom, 1971 to 1992

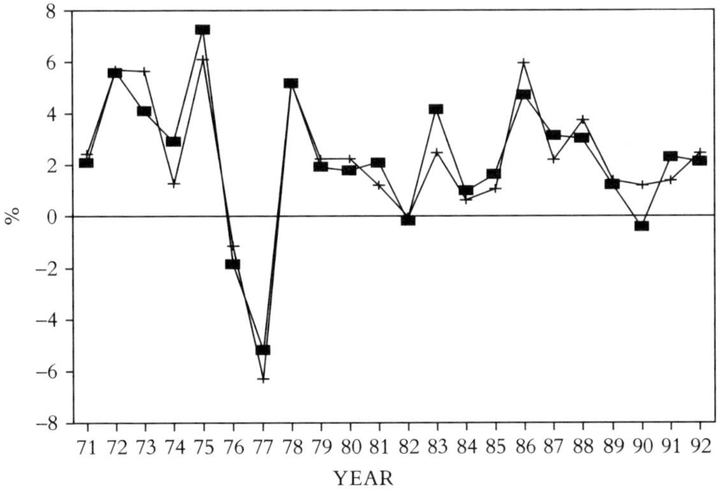

+ = IE/EE; RPI (UKD8/EE; RPI)
■ = (IE + LIS)/WE; RPI ((UKD8 + LIS)/UKD5; RPI)
See note on Figure 2.2a for LIS, and Appendix 2B for EE and RPI, respectively.

Figure 2.12. Change in the Real Wage Rate (%), United States, 1971 to 1992

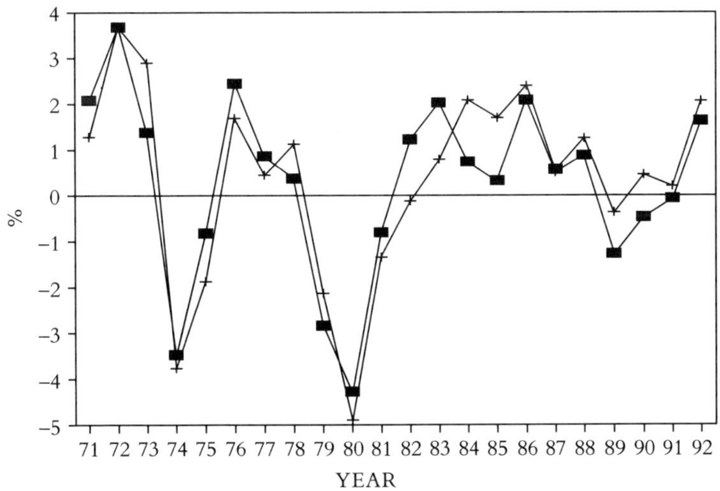

■ = IE/EE; CPI, where EE = Employees (Farm + Nonfarm) + RAF, RAF = Resident armed forces (USD12/{USD7 + (T30, T95 & T41 *ERP*)}; USD3)
+ = (IE + LIS)/(WE + RAF); CPI ((USD12 + LIS)/(T30 *ERP*); USD3)
See note on Figure 2.3a for LIS.

Figure 2.13. Change in the Real Wage Rate (%), Japan, 1971 to 1991

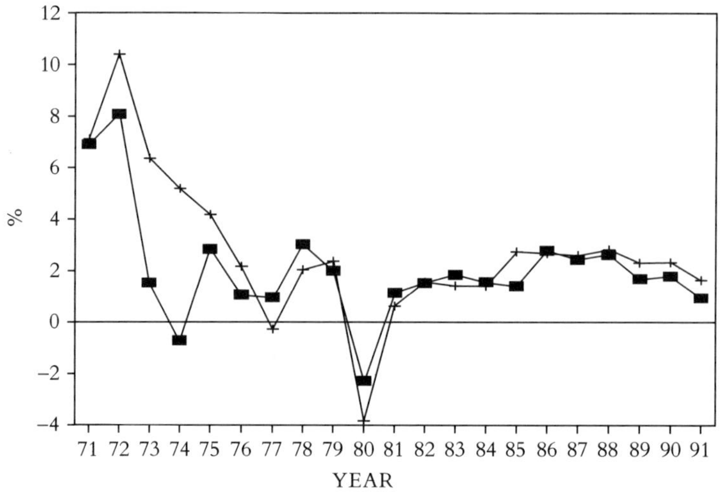

■ = IE/EE; CPI (JPD5/(T3–1 *RH*); JPD4)
+ = (EI + LIS)/WE; CPI ((JPD5 + LIS)/(T3–1 *RH*); JPD4)
See note on Figure 2.4a for LIS.

Japan

In Figure 2.13, a similar kind of symmetrical change of the real wage rate for the employees' case in Japan is observed in the 1970s (with some exceptions). The growth rate is rather stable—around 2 percent in the 1980s—except for 1980, the year of the second sudden oil price increase. The two estimates are similar, especially since 1981; however, they have a great difference, especially in the first half of the 1970s. This is due to the relatively high labor income from self-employment (LIS) during this period, which is partly caused by the relatively high income from self-employment (IS) itself for the years 1972 to 1974[19] and partly by the effect of low profit rates for imputation of self-employment income for 1974 to 1977.[20]

The Relationship Between the Estimates with and Without LIS

United Kingdom

The direction of movements of the labor shares between these two kinds of estimates is similar in the United Kingdom. However, the gaps between these increased in the 1980s, reflecting the greater increase in the number of self-employed from 2 (1980) to 3.3 million (1990).

United States

The same is true of the direction of movements between the two estimates in the United States. However, the gaps between these are fairly narrow, particularly in 1980 to 1983. This is possible to explain as a combined effect of the sluggish situation of noncorporates in those years and the steady increase in income from employment.[21]

Japan

The Japanese labor share estimates have different characteristics. The gaps between the two kinds of estimates are similar before 1976, but from 1977 on they become narrower. This reflects the drastic change in various factors related to self-employed businesses.[22] However, the direction of the movements of the labor share is similar, though there are some exceptions (particularly for 1973 and 1980).[23]

Growth rates of the real wage rate estimates are also similar, although there are some years when large differences are apparent, especially 1982 to 1985 for the United States and 1972 to 1975 for Japan (see Figures 2.11 to 2.13).

FACTORS CONDITIONING INTERPRETATIONS

Interpreting the above data should take into account the following conditions. The first such consideration relates to the fact that trough and peak years are adjusted for GDP and GNP. The trough and peak years in the cyclical indicator (coincident) were not always the same as adjusted trough and peak years in each country. Mostly they coincided with each other, with a couple of exceptional years in each country. Some of these exceptional years may be caused by differences in estimation coverage. The trough and peak years for manufacturing are not always the same as those for the whole economy. This is true of the business sector and the production industry. A partial index is not always coincident with a composite one. Therefore, an exceptional year is sometimes not an exception but a due course. It is called an exception only from the viewpoint of the whole economy.

Second, the disturbing effects of the first oil shock, the worldwide inflation in the early 1970s, and the second oil shock (1979 to 1981) should be considered. Some observations could be biased due to the effect of these disturbances. For example, during those years (particularly in 1973, 1974, 1979, and 1980), the volumes of stock valuation adjustment in Japan were greater enough to distort and sometimes to conceal the overall real change.[24]

The third factor relates to a few years at both ends of the observation period. The first and the last few years should be considered in relation to the years prior to 1970 and the most recent years, respectively. Some caution needs to be exercised in establishing a pattern.

Finally, the specific economic situation in each country should be considered. For example, the weakness of the business cycle in the mid-1980s in the United Kingdom, the 1977 recession in Japan, the great structural changes in the first half of the 1970s in Japan, and so on.[25]

Considering these conditions makes it possible to discount most of the irregular results that might seem to distort the overall pattern.

STYLIZED FACTS AND SOME EXPLANATIONS OF THESE FACTS

Stylized Facts

Through our comparative study of the United Kingdom, the United States, and Japan, the following stylized facts can be established:

First, there is no agreement on whether the labor share moves countercyclically or procyclically in the business cycle. However, the labor share increases in the first year of contraction and decreases in the first year of expansion, though there are some exceptions. This pattern was strongly supported by the longer observation for Japan (1955 to 1985) and for the United Kingdom (1955 to 1982), respectively.

Second, the profit rate moves procyclically with the business cycle. However, the cyclical change of the profit rate does not always coincide with the trough or peak years in the business cycle.

Third, labor productivity moves procyclically. In particular, a symmetrical change in productivity growth in the phase of the business cycle is observed. Productivity (labor productivity per person employed) sharply increases in the first year of expansion in terms of the growth rate and decreases in the first year of contraction.

Fourth, the real wage rate has no common feature, despite the fact that its symmetrical change in the phase of the business cycle is clear in the United States.[26]

Lastly, the labor shares with and without LIS imputed from self-employment income are almost parallel except for Japan, and their movements are also similar, though they move differently for some years. These similar movements hold true of the two kinds of estimate of the real wage rate.

Summary Table

Some stylized facts are stated in relation to the first years of contraction and expansion. Tables 2.2 and 2.3 are summaries of the number of observations in this relation.

Table 2.2 shows the number of observations with respect to labor share, profit rate, and productivity, and Table 2.3 shows the number of observations with respect to the real wage rate. On counting the number of observations with respect to productivity, the average growth rate in (labor) productivity is deducted as the growth trend, which reflects technical progress and so on.

As was stated above in the stylized facts, the number of observations with regard to the first three variables (labor share, profit rate, and productivity) seems to appear with regularity, respectively. However, regarding the real wage rate, there is no common feature between the three countries. The contingency tables obtained from Table 2.2 show the significance level at which the null hypothesis is rejected.

Contingency Table

Table 2.4a shows that the null hypothesis with regard to the change of labor's share is rejected at the 5 percent significance level. This means that the

Table 2.2. Summary of Number of Observations

Country	First Year of Contraction	Annual Change: Labor Share (IE/GDP) Positive	Profit Rate Decrease	Productivity (GDPC/WE) Negative[a]
Number of observations in the first contraction year:				
United Kingdom	4	4	4	4
United States	3	2	3	3
Japan	4	4	3	3
Number of observations in the first expansion year:				
United Kingdom	4	3	3	4
United States	3	2	3	3
Japan	5	3	4	4

Note: IE/GDP = Income from employment/Gross domestic product
GDPC/WE = Gross domestic product at constant price/Workforce in employment
a. On counting the number of observations, the average growth rate in (labor) productivity is deducted as the growth trend, which reflects technical progress and so on. The average rates in percentages are 2.04 (United Kingdom), 0.70 (United States), and 3.15 (Japan).

Table 2.3. Summary of Number of Observations

Country	First Year of Contraction	Real Wage Rate[a]: Decrease IE/EE Case	Decrease (IE + LIS)/WE Case
Number of observations in the first contraction year:			
United Kingdom	4	0 (3)	0 (3)
United States	3	3 (3)	3 (3)
Japan	4	2 (3)	1 (2)
Number of observations in the first expansion year:			
United Kingdom	4	2 (1)	2 (1)
United States	3	3 (3)	3 (3)
Japan	5	5 (5)	5 (3)

Note: IE/EE = Income from employment/Employees in employment
(IE + LIS)/WE = (Income from employment + Labor income from self-employment)/Workforce in employment
a. The number in parentheses shows that, on counting the number of observations, the average growth rate of the real wages is deducted. The average rates in percentages are

IE/EE case: 2.19 (United Kingdom), 0.25 (United States), and 1.54 (Japan for 1973 to 1991),
(IE + LIS)/WE case: 2.11 (United Kingdom), 0.34 (United States), and 2.66 (Japan for 1976 to 1991).

The United Kingdom shows very poor fit in relation to the real wage rate, so the table is just for reference. The United States shows the complete fit.

direction of change in labor's share is not independent from the first year of contraction or the first year of expansion. In Tables 2.4b and 2.4c the null hypothesis with regard to the profit rate and productivity is rejected at the half percent significance level, respectively. So the direction of changes in both the profit rate and productivity are not independent from the first year of contraction or the first year of expansion.

Table 2.4. Contingency Table on the Symmetrical Change of Macroeconomic Variables in the Business Cycle

a. Annual change of labor's share (ρ_1) in national income

		Expected: Positive (+)	Expected: Negative (−)	Total
Observed	First year of contraction	$O = 10$ ($E = 6.7$)	$O = 1$ ($E = 4.3$)	$r_1 = 11$
	First year of expansion	$O = 4$ ($E = 7.3$)	$O = 8$ ($E = 4.7$)	$r_2 = 12$
	Total	$c_1 = 14$	$c_2 = 9$	$N = 23$

Notes: (1) Expected changes as percentages of all observed years covered = 78.3.
(2) $x^2(1) = 7.97$.
(3) $E(i, j) = (r_i c_i)/N$, and

$$x^2 = \sum_i \sum_j \frac{(O_{ij} - E_{ij})^2}{E_{ij}} \sim x^2(1),$$

where E = Expected frequency,
O = Observed frequency,
r = Row,
c = Column,
N = Total number of observations,
$i, j = 1 \sim 2$.

(4) This is a combined table of three countries (United Kingdom, United States, and Japan). Considering the degree of freedom as three, the tabulated x^2 value at the 5 percent level (0.05) is 7.81. Our computed value of x^2 (7.97) is greater than this value, so the null hypothesis is rejected at this 5 percent significance level. This means that the direction of change in labor's share is not independent from the first year of contraction or the first year of expansion.

(5) I owe the idea for this table to Professor Kent Matthews, who suggested that I apply the chi-square test and kindly made contingency tables for me from Table 2.2. See Moore (1969) for a chi-square test (for example, p. 405), Table 25–1, on turning point forecasts, and see Everitt (1977) for the explanation of contingency tables, particularly for his arguments on combined tables (Section 2.7 of Chapter 2) and small expected frequencies (Section 3.3 of Chapter 3). I also received some helpful suggestions from my colleague Professor Hiromi Ando.

b. Change in the profit rate (π)

		Expected: Positive (+)	Expected: Negative (−)	Total
Observed	First year of contraction	$O = 1$ ($E = 5.3$)	$O = 10$ ($E = 5.7$)	$r_1 = 11$
	First year of expansion	$O = 10$ ($E = 5.7$)	$O = 2$ ($E = 6.3$)	$r_2 = 12$
	Total	$c_2 = 11$	$c_1 = 12$	$N = 23$

Notes: (1) Expected changes as percentages of all observed years covered = 87.0.
(2) $x^2(1) = 12.91$.
(3) This is also a combined table of three countries. At the half percent level (0.005) the tabulated x^2 value for three degrees of freedom is 12.83. The statistic x^2 is 12.91, so the null hypothesis is rejected at this half percent significance level.

c. Annual change in labor productivity (μ)

		Expected: Positive (+)	Expected: Negative (−)	Total
Observed	First year of contraction	$O = 1$ ($E = 5.7$)	$O = 10$ ($E = 5.3$)	$r_1 = 11$
	First year of expansion	$O = 11$ ($E = 6.3$)	$O = 1$ ($E = 5.7$)	$r_2 = 12$
	Total	$c_2 = 12$	$c_1 = 11$	$N = 23$

Notes: (1) Expected changes as percentages of all observed years covered = 91.3.
(2) $x^2(1) = 15.43$.
(3) The tabulated x^2 value with three degrees of freedom at the half percent level (0.005) is 12.83 as in above b. The null hypothesis is rejected at this half percent significance level.

Table 2.4. (continued)

		Expected		
		Negative (−) for π & μ Positive (+) for ρ_1	Positive (+) for π & μ Negative (−) for ρ_1	Total
d. All combined: ρ_1, π, and μ				
Observed	First year of contraction	$O = 30$ ($E = 17.7$)	$O = 3$ ($E = 15.3$)	$r_1 = 33$
	First year of expansion	$O = 7$ ($E = 19.3$)	$O = 29$ ($E = 16.7$)	$r_2 = 36$
	Total	$c_1 = 37$	$c_2 = 32$	$N = 69$

Notes: (1) Expected changes as percentages of all observed years covered = 85.5.
(2) $x^2(1) = 35.33$.
(3) This is a combined table of a, b, and c. This table is just for reference. The tabulated x^2 values with nine degrees of freedom at (0.05), (0.01), and (0.001) levels are 16.91, 21.66, and 27.87, respectively. Considering the result of contingency table a, it is difficult to judge this significance level. However, it would be safe to say that the null hypothesis is rejected at least at the 5 percent significance level.

Observing these results, a symmetrical change of the labor share between the first years of contraction and expansion seems to be fairly clear, and this symmetrical change in the business cycle is more robust for the profit rate and productivity.

However, there are a couple of factors conditioning the value of these findings. First are the limited period of observation (twenty-two years) and the limited number of countries (three advanced countries). Second is the reliability of estimates. Regarding this question, see the section above on Factors Conditioning Interpretation.

Some Explanations of the Stylized Facts

These stylized facts are explained in this section, starting with an explanation of a symmetrical change in productivity, which affects the other explanations that follow it.

A Symmetrical Change in Productivity Growth

It is possible to explain this symmetrical change in productivity growth as a combined effect of changes in *capacity utilization* and in *overhead* labor. Productivity (output per worker) is a positive function of capacity utilization in the short run. In early contraction employers cannot release or shed a proportional number of workers between direct and overhead labor in the face of falling production because the need for overhead workers does not decline as output falls. In contrast, in early expansion, a proportional number of direct and overhead workers is not necessary; the need for overhead workers is small in the face of increasing production. In addition, capacity utilization increases in the business expansion and decreases in the business contraction. These facts play an important role in explaining why productivity rises rapidly in early expansion and falls rapidly in early contraction. Taking into consideration technical progress, productivity does not necessary fall, but its growth rate does decline.

Movements of the Labor Share

Movements of the labor share are explained as follows. Writing W and Y, for wages (paid) and output, the relative share of labor (ρ_1) is generally defined as

$$\rho_1 \equiv W/Y. \tag{2.1}$$

Wages and output are respectively expressed by identities:

$$W \equiv \omega_m L, \text{ and}$$

$$Y \equiv e\mu L,$$

where

ω_m = money wage rate,

L = employed labor force,

e = price level, and

μ = labor productivity.

Substituting these W and Y into (2.1), we have

$$\rho_1 = \omega_m / e\mu.$$

From this, we derive the growth rate equation

$$\hat{\rho}_1 = \hat{\omega}_m - (\hat{e} + \hat{\mu}), \tag{2.2}$$

where $\dot{\rho}_1$ and $\hat{\rho}_1$ represent $d\rho_1/dt$ and $\dot{\rho}_1/\rho_1$, respectively.

By using equation (2.2), movements in the labor share are theoretically explained as a combined effect of changes of *capacity utilization* and of *wage lag*. The labor share moves countercyclically in the following case. In the expansion process, productivity grows as capacity utilization improves. If productivity growth plus price increases are greater than the wage increase that lags behind changes in national income ($\hat{\omega}_m < \hat{e} + \hat{\mu}$), the labor share decreases. In the contraction period this relationship becomes reverse due to slow or negative productivity growth, a relatively low price increase, and a relatively high increase of wages because of wages lagging behind changes in national income ($\hat{\omega}_m > \hat{e} + \hat{\mu}$). As a result, the labor share increases.

The labor share moves procyclically when the reverse relationship to the above occurs in the expansion and the contraction processes, respectively. However, we may safely conclude that what actually happens is a matter of fact.[27]

A Symmetrical Change in the Labor Share Between the First Years of Expansion and Contraction

A symmetrical change in the labor share between the first years of expansion and contraction can be explained as a combined effect of *wage lag*[28] on the one hand and the *symmetrical change in productivity growth* on the other, as explained above.

Wages lag behind changes in national income. The wage increase is not fast enough to keep up with rapid productivity growth in early expansion, and the wage increase is not slow enough to keep up with negative or relatively low productivity growth in early contraction. Therefore, the decrease in the labor share in the first year of expansion results from the rapid growth of productivity (which is almost at its cyclical peak rate of growth), which exceeds the rate of growth in wages. Conversely, the increase in the labor share in the first year of contraction is made due to a rate of wage growth that is faster than that in productivity.

Procyclical Movements in the Profit Rate

Procyclical movements of the profit rate in the business cycle might be generally expected. However, we must clearly understand the difference between microeconomy level and macroeconomy level. These have the possibility of moving differently with respect to each other. This is caused by the differences in profit calculation of business corporations between the national income base and corporate accounting principles (refer to note 16).

The Real Wage Rate

The real wage rate has no stylized fact in relation to the business cycle. The change of the real wage rate may depend on various kinds of conditions such as the economic growth rate, productivity growth, and customary wage contracts. Therefore, there needs to be a more specific analysis of each country. For example, in the United Kingdom the real wage rate changes around 2 percent during the observation period from 1970 to 1992. The United States has a great change in its growth rate in the business cycle but has a symmetrical change of the real wage rate between the first years of expansion and contraction. Japan's growth rate stabilized during the years 1981 to 1991.

The Relationship Between the Estimates with and Without LIS

If estimates both with and without LIS are in parallel and move in the same direction, an estimate without LIS (employees' case calculated by IE/GDP or IE/GNP) can be a rough substitute for the other. However, when the economy undergoes a great structural change, especially in self-employed businesses like Japan in the 1970s, an estimate with LIS is necessary.

APPENDIX 2A: METHODS OF IMPUTATION AND THEIR VALIDITY

This appendix considers two basic methods of imputation and the validity of the estimate for Japan and the United Kingdom.

Two Basic Methods

The first method is the *asset basis.* This method imputes to self-employed businesses some assumed rate of profit on capital and treats LIS (their labor income) as a residual. One of the simple assumptions made in this chapter is that the capital stock of unincorporated enterprises yields the same profit rate as incorporated enterprises.

The second method is the *labor basis*, which imputes to self-employed persons some amount of wages (or salaries), treating the remainder of their income as property income. The simplest way of doing this is to assume that they earn wages (or salaries) equivalent to employees' average income.[29]

Validity

The validity of the estimates between these two bases is theoretically judged by the degree of competition between labor and capital markets. If the labor market is more competitive than the capital market, an estimate based on the labor basis is more reliable than one based on the asset basis. In the reverse case, the asset basis rather than the labor basis becomes the more reliable method of imputation. Because in the competitive market, we can assume the same wage rate and the same profit rate on capital.

However, the realities of self-employed businesses vary from country to country: their size and weight in the economy, industry, age, and sex distribution of self-employed people; business conditions (growing, stable or declining); and so on. An arbitrary assumption is more or less inevitable on both bases in imputation.

Earlier work supported the labor basis for Japan (Iyoda, 1979, estimated years 1955 to 1976) and the United Kingdom (Iyoda 1985, estimated years 1950 to 1982). Later, however, some difficulty was found for the labor basis estimate since 1975 of Japan (Iyoda 1987, estimated years 1950 to 1985). This is due to the effect of the standard change to 1980 (bench year) in the New System of the National Accounts (NSNA). As a result, about a third of family workers became employees (Iyoda 1987, p. 3 n. 2).

In addition to this, self-employed businesses have undergone a drastic change since the first oil shock. For example, average earning ratios of the self-employed to employees in percentage terms decreased from 88.9 (1975) to only 60.6 (1985). Aging of self-employed persons was rapid: percentages of self-employed persons of fifty-five years and over increased from 31.1 (1975) to 36.0 (1985). During the same period, the same percentage in agriculture, for instance, rapidly increased from 43.3 to 62.8 (Iyoda 1988, tables 3 and 4).

For the United Kingdom there was a good fit for 1954 to 1979 between two estimates based on respective methods during the observation period 1950 to 1982. I chose the labor basis as the more appropriate method. First, the larger gap between the two estimates was possibly due to my estimate of net capital stock by sector of the early 1950s for the calculation of labor share. Second, it is difficult to assume that two broad groups of capital gain the same profits rate, taking into account the risk and tax elements (the limitation of liability and the tax regime between two groups are different).[30]

In Iyoda (1985), I calculated LIS in imputation based on labor basis, on the assumption that self-employed persons earn roughly equivalent wages to average earnings of nonmanual workers (for an assumption in detail, see the paper). Considering that there was a larger increase in the number of self-employed businesses during the 1980s in the United Kingdom, it is unclear whether the same method on the labor basis still applies to it.

APPENDIX 2B: DATA

Datastream

(As of October 25, and November 1, 1993)

United Kingdom

(1)	UKOPER . . E	INDEX	Output per person employed (whole economy) SADJ
(2)	UKOPERIPE	INDEX	Output per person employed (production industries) SADJ
(3)	UKGNPMKTB	£Mil	GNP market prices CURA
(4)	UKGDPMKTB	£Mil	GDP market prices CURA
(5)	UKEMPLABE	000	Workforce in employment in the United Kingdom SADJ
(6)	UKGDPIPME	INDEX	Implicit price deflator of GDP (market prices) SADJ
(7)	UKCOININ	INDEX	CSO coincident indicator
(8)	UKINCEMPB	£Mil	Income from employment CURA
(9)	UKGRRAIC	%	Gross rate of return on capital employed—all industries and commercial companies
(10)	UKNRRAIC	%	Net above
(11)	UKGRRMAN	%	Gross rate of return on capital employed—manufacturing companies
(12)	UKNRRMAN	%	Net above

United States

(1)	USGNP . . . B	$Bln	GNP (annual rate) CURA
(2)	USCOININ	INDEX	U.S. Department of Commerce's coincident indicator

(3)	USCP. . . . E	INDEX	CPI (all urban consumers) SADJ
(4)	USIPDGNPE	INDEX	Implicit price deflator of the GNP SADJ
(5)	USGDP. . . B	$Bln	GDP (annual rate) CURA
(6)	USIPDGDPE	INDEX	Implicit price deflator of the GDP SADJ
(7)	USEMPTOTE	000	Total civilian employment SADJ
(8)	USEMPGOVE	000	Employees employed by the government SADJ
(9)	USCPIW . . F	INDEX	CPI—all items: wages earners and clerical workers
(10)	USOPERATE	%	Capacity utilization rate (all industries)
(11)	USOPHNFNE	INDEX	Output per all-employee hour—nonfinancial corporate sector
(12)	USCOMEMPB	$Bln	Compensation of employees (annual rate) CURA
(13)	USOPHPBSE	INDEX	Output per hour of all persons—private business sector SADJ
(14)	USCPTPRFB	$Bln	Corporate profits after tax excluding IVA and CC adjusted (annual rate)
(15)	USPIFARMB	$Bln	Proprietor's income with IVA and CC adjusted—farm (annual rate) CURA
(16)	USPINFRMB	$Bln	Above—nonfarm (annual rate) CURA
(17)	USCPICTOB	$Bln	Corporate profits with IVA and CC adjusted —total (annual rate) CURA
(18)	USPROFBTB	$Bln	Corporate profits before tax excluding IVA and CC adjusted (annual rate)
(19)	USLABCOSE	INDEX	Unit labor costs in manufacturing SADJ
(20)	USCPANNL	%	CPI—annual inflation rate
(21)	USCAPMANE	%	Capacity utilization rate (manufacturing)
(22)	USULCPBSE	INDEX	Unit labor costs—private business sector SADJ
(23)	USLABFRCE	000	Total civilian labor force SADJ
(24)	USUNEMP.E	000	Total unemployment level SADJ
(25)	USEMPPRVE	000	Employment in total private industry SADJ

Japan

(1)	JPGNP . . . B	YBln	GNP (at annual rates) CURA
(2)	JPIPDGNPE	INDEX	Implicit price deflator of the GNP SADJ
(3)	JPTOTEMPF	000	Total level of employment NADJ
(4)	JPCNPRICF	INDEX	CPI (national measure) NADJ
(5)	JPCOMEMPB	YBln	Compensation of employees (at annual rates) CURA
(6)	JPCOININ	%	Diffusion index (coincident indicator)
(7)	JPMNULABE	INDEX	Unit labor cost index for manufacturing industries

(8)	JPPRODVTF	INDEX	Labor productivity index—all industries
(9)	JPNETPRFB	YBln	Current profits of incorporated businesses
(10)	JPOPPROFB	YBln	Operating profits of incorporated businesses
(11)	JPOCGVOLG	INDEX	Gross domestic product—volume

Symbols[31]

(Ninth character key in *Datastream* code)
B Current price (seasonally adjusted) CURA
E Seasonally adjusted SADJ
F Not seasonally adjusted NADJ
G Volume (seasonally adjusted) VOLA

Others

United Kingdom

DATA SOURCE ABBREVIATION

NAE *National Account and Expenditure*, Central Statistical Office (CSO). London: HMSO.
NA *United Kingdom National Accounts*, CSO. London: HMSO.
ETAS *Economic Trends: Annual Supplements*, CSO. London: HMSO.
ET *Economic Trends*, CSO. London: HMSO.
EG *Employment Gazette*, Department of Employment. London: HMSO.

DATA

NCS (net capital stock by sector and type of asset at current replacement cost):
T11.11 *NAE* 1981 for 1970 to 1973,
T11.7 *NA* 1985 for 1974 to 1981, and
T14.7 *NA* 1993 for 1982 to 1992.

IS (income from self-employment), GTP (gross trading profits of companies), and GTS (gross trading surplus of public corporations) (factor incomes after providing for stock appreciation):
T1.3 *NA* 1992 for 1970, and
T1.4 *NA* 1993 for 1971 to 1992.

ULC (unit labor costs: wages and salaries per unit of output, 1985 = 100):
T24 *ETAS* 1993 for 1970 to 1989, and
T5.8 *EG* September 1993 for 1990 to 1992.

EE (employees in employment including HM forces but excluding government trainees):
T1.12 *NIE* 1982 for 1970 to 1981, and
T17.1 *NA* 1993 for 1982 to 1992.

RPI (retail price index, 1985 = 100):
T25 *ETAS* 1993 for 1970 to 1991, and
T26 *ET* May 1993 for 1992.

United States

DATA SOURCE ABBREVIATION

ERP *Economic Report of the President*, Council of Economic Advisers. Washington: U.S. Government Printing Office.

SCB *Survey of Current Business*, Bureau of Economic Analysis of the U.S. Department of Commerce. Washington: U.S. Government Printing Office.

DATA

PBT (profits before income taxes)[32] and SE (stockholders' equity) (all manufacturing corporations):

T88 *ERP* 1993 for 1970 to 1991.

The labor force—

WE (workforce in employment), and RAF (resident armed forces):

T30 *ERP* 1993 for 1970 to 1992.

FE (farm employees):

T95 *ERP* 1993 for 1970 to 1990, the number in 1990 for 1991 to 1992.

NFE (nonfarm employees):

T41 *ERP* 1993 for 1970 to 1991, extrapolated for 1992.

NCS (current cost net stock of fixed nonresidential private capital by regal form of organization):

T6 *SCB* January 1992 for 1970 to 1988, and

T6 *SCB* September 1993 for 1989 to 1992.

Japan

DATA SOURCE ABBREVIATION

ANA *Annual Report on National Accounts*, Economic Planning Agency (EPA). Tokyo: Printing Bureau, Ministry of Finance.

CSP Capital Stock of Private Enterprises, Economic Institute of Economic Planning Agency

RH *Rodo Hakusho [White Paper on Labor]*, Ministry of Labor. Tokyo: Nihon Rodo-Kenkyu Kiko.

DATA

National income

GDP at Market Prices:

Part 1[2]IV, 1 *ANA* 1993 for 1970 to 1992.

IS (unincorporated; farm and nonfarm), and PI (profits of incorporated enterprises):

Part 1[2]IV, 2 *ANA* 1993 for 1970 to 1992.

GCS (Gross capital stock by industry at 1985 average replacement costs):

T1 *CSP* 1993 for 1970 to 1992.

The labor force

EE (employees in employment) and WE (workforce in employment)

T3–1 *RH* 1993 for 1970 to 1992.

Table 2.5. Coincident Indicator (JP: Diffusion Index), United Kingdom, United States, Japan, 1970 to 1992

Year	United Kingdom	Cyclical Trough and Peak	United States	Cyclical Trough and Peak	Japan	Cyclical Trough and Peak
1970	100.80		82.1		56.5	
1971	95.69		82.3		39.6	T
1972	97.47	T (Adj)	88.9		87.5	
1973	108.17	P	96.0	P	83.3	P
1974	103.46		94.1		14.4	T
1975	94.37	T	86.3	T	50.0	
1976	96.27		92.3		76.5	P
1977	99.09		98.7		47.7	T
1978	102.77		106.7		86.4	
1979	108.70	P	110.8	P	83.7	P
1980	99.04		107.2		42.4	
1981	93.69	T	107.3		53.4	
1982	94.01		100.0	T	28.0	
1983	99.03	P (Adj)	101.9		69.3	T (Adj)
1984	101.82	T (Adj)	112.2		79.9	
1985	98.17		116.3		50.8	P
1986	96.21		119.0		34.1	T
1987	100.42		123.5		82.6	
1988	107.07	P	129.1	P (Adj)	76.5	
1989	106.59		132.2		67.0	
1990	103.35		131.7		68.9	
1991	95.12		124.5	T (Adj)	31.8	P
1992	94.63	T	123.6		16.3	

Note: United Kingdom—Central Statistical Office.
United States—Department of Commerce.
Japan—Economic Planning Agency.
Adj = adjusted

Table 2.6. Share of Labor in National Income (percent), United Kingdom, 1970 to 1992

Year	(IE[a]+LIS)/GNP (1)	IE[a]/GNP (2)	IE[a]/GDP (3)	Annual Rate of Change (1)	(2)	(3)
1970	64.59	58.35	59.12			
1971	63.92	57.44	57.66	−1.04	−1.55	−2.47
1972	65.07	58.03	58.85	1.81	1.03	2.07
1973	65.76	58.05	59.01	1.05	0.03	0.26
1974	68.40	61.36	61.86	4.01	5.69	4.83
1975	70.77	64.17	64.02	3.47	4.58	3.50
1976	68.33	61.51	61.05	−3.45	−4.13	−4.65
1977	64.95	59.20	58.84	−4.95	−3.77	−3.61
1978	64.08	58.37	58.27	−1.34	−1.39	−0.97
1979	63.75	58.10	58.38	−0.51	−0.47	0.19
1980	65.33	59.49	59.25	2.48	2.40	1.48
1981	64.55	58.45	58.41	−1.19	−1.75	−1.42
1982	62.77	56.63	56.81	−2.76	−3.12	−2.73
1983	61.27	55.27	55.65	−2.39	−2.39	−2.04
1984	61.52	54.94	55.75	0.41	−0.60	0.18
1985	61.07	54.74	55.09	−0.73	−0.37	−1.19
1986	61.88	54.53	55.19	1.33	−0.38	0.18
1987	61.35	53.81	54.28	−0.86	−1.33	−1.63
1988	61.80	53.72	54.23	0.73	−0.16	−0.11
1989	63.45	54.58	54.94	2.68	1.60	1.31
1990	66.18	56.51	56.68	4.30	3.54	3.17
1991	66.16	57.19	57.18	−0.04	1.21	0.88
1992	65.13	56.65	57.16	−1.55	−0.94	−0.04

a. Income from employment.

Table 2.7. Share of Labor in National Income (percent), United States, 1970 to 1992

Year	(IE[a]+LIS)/GNP (1)	IE[a]/GNP (2)	IE[a]/GDP (3)	Annual Rate of Change (1)	(2)	(3)
1970	65.95	60.81	61.20			
1971	64.55	59.70	60.12	−2.13	−1.83	−1.76
1972	64.71	59.76	60.19	0.25	0.10	0.12
1973	65.16	59.69	60.25	0.70	−1.12	0.10
1974	65.83	60.48	61.14	1.03	1.33	1.47
1975	64.39	59.37	59.86	−2.20	−1.85	−2.08
1976	64.04	59.32	59.89	−0.53	−0.08	0.50
1977	63.46	59.02	59.64	−0.92	−0.50	−0.43
1978	63.62	59.13	59.70	0.26	0.17	0.11
1979	63.89	59.36	60.13	0.43	0.40	0.71
1980	64.10	59.97	60.72	0.33	1.02	0.99
1981	63.23	59.26	59.91	−1.37	−1.19	−1.35
1982	64.09	60.26	60.83	1.36	1.69	1.55
1983	62.52	59.09	59.60	−2.44	−1.93	−2.03
1984	62.55	58.58	58.96	0.04	−0.86	−1.08
1985	62.97	58.78	59.00	0.67	0.35	0.07
1986	63.59	59.00	59.12	0.99	0.37	0.21
1987	63.92	59.38	59.44	0.53	0.65	0.54
1988	63.71	59.52	59.61	−0.33	0.23	0.29
1989	63.21	58.86	59.04	−0.78	−1.10	−0.96
1990	63.54	59.22	59.46	0.52	0.61	0.70
1991	63.80	59.31	59.45	0.41	0.14	−0.01
1992	63.96	59.25	59.32	0.24	−0.10	−0.22

a. Income from employment.

Table 2.8. Share of Labor in National Income (percent), Japan, 1970 to 1991

Year	(IE[a]+LIS)/GNP (1)	IE[a]/GNP (2)	IE[a]/GDP (3)	Annual Rate of Change (1)	(2)	(3)
1970	51.82	42.09	41.88			
1971	54.33	45.30	45.15	4.84	7.63	7.80
1972	54.99	45.88	45.74	1.23	1.28	1.30
1973	55.49	45.42	45.21	0.91	−1.00	−1.15
1974	60.58	50.42	50.10	9.16	11.01	10.81
1975	63.29	53.47	53.31	4.48	6.05	6.41
1976	63.70	54.15	54.03	0.65	1.27	1.34
1977	62.44	54.19	54.12	−1.97	0.08	0.17
1978	60.70	53.20	53.19	−2.80	−1.84	−1.71
1979	60.35	53.03	53.00	−0.57	−0.32	−0.35
1980	59.11	53.34	53.23	−2.05	0.58	0.44
1981	58.92	53.83	53.67	−0.33	0.94	0.81
1982	59.10	54.23	54.23	0.32	0.74	1.06
1983	59.79	55.49	55.54	1.15	2.31	2.41
1984	58.54	54.82	54.88	−2.10	−1.20	−1.19
1985	57.90	53.76	53.91	−1.10	−1.94	−1.77
1986	57.91	54.10	54.28	0.02	0.64	0.69
1987	57.56	53.81	54.08	−0.60	−0.53	−0.36
1988	56.95	53.49	53.81	−1.06	−0.59	−0.50
1989	57.08	53.79	54.13	0.24	0.56	0.60
1990	57.58	54.55	54.88	0.87	1.41	1.39
1991	58.36	55.47	55.84	1.36	1.69	1.74

a. Income from employment.

Table 2.9. Rate of Profits (percent), United Kingdom, 1970 to 1992

Year	Companies	Companies and Public Corporations	Rate of Return on Capital Employed (Manufacturing Companies) Gross	Net	Rate of Return on Capital Employed (All Industries and Commercial Companies) Gross	Net
1970	12.63	10.46	7.9	7.9	8.8	8.7
1971	13.24	10.76	7.2	6.8	9.0	9.0
1972	12.67	10.44	7.9	8.1	9.2	9.3
1973	11.24	9.56	7.9	8.1	8.7	8.8
1974	7.66	6.48	5.3	4.3	6.2	5.0
1975	7.37	6.29	4.4	2.7	5.6	4.0
1976	7.88	7.16	4.7	3.2	5.9	4.4
1977	11.96	9.76	6.4	5.8	8.1	7.5
1978	12.13	9.84	6.7	6.2	8.6	8.2
1979	11.38	9.04	5.6	4.5	8.3	7.7
1980	10.05	8.22	4.3	2.5	7.7	6.7
1981	9.26	8.08	3.8	1.5	7.4	6.3
1982	11.10	9.61	4.9	3.4	8.4	7.8
1983	13.84	11.58	5.4	4.2	9.4	9.3
1984	13.47	11.55	5.3	4.0	10.1	10.5
1985	15.49	12.69	6.1	5.4	10.6	11.2
1986	12.84	11.37	6.4	5.9	9.4	9.2
1987	14.07	12.13	6.3	5.7	9.6	9.7
1988	13.51	11.71	7.2	7.2	10.0	10.4
1989	11.58	10.65	7.1	7.2	9.6	9.7
1990	10.21	9.52	7.3	7.3	8.8	8.3
1991	9.76	9.05	6.8	6.4	8.3	7.6
1992	10.26	9.50	6.8	6.3	8.3	7.6

Table 2.10. Rate of Profits (percent), United States, 1970 to 1992

Year	(Profits Before Income Taxes)/ (Stockholders' Equity) (All Manufacturing Corporations)	(Profits of Incorporated Enterprises)/ (Current Cost Net Stock) (Corporations)
1970	15.85	11.96
1971	16.67	12.70
1972	18.60	13.04
1973	21.99	12.95
1974	23.32	9.66
1975	18.87	9.95
1976	22.67	10.96
1977	23.17	11.79
1978	24.51	11.82
1979	25.68	10.44
1980	21.82	7.94
1981	21.33	7.17
1982	14.05	5.58
1983	16.38	7.59
1984	19.16	8.96
1985	15.82	9.02
1986	14.78	8.31
1987	19.20	9.38
1988	22.57	10.05
1989	18.90	9.46
1990	15.29	9.46
1991	9.38	8.97
1992		9.70

Table 2.11. Rate of Profits (percent), Japan, 1970 to 1992

Year	((Net) Operating Profits)/ (Gross Capital Stock) (Incorporated Enterprises)	(Profits)/(Gross Capital Stock) (Incorporated Enterprises)
1970	6.89	8.86
1971	5.55	7.07
1972	5.91	7.10
1973	8.76	7.12
1974	8.03	5.51
1975	5.91	4.32
1976	7.05	5.13
1977	6.72	5.69
1978	7.18	8.01
1979	9.08	8.21
1980	9.89	7.83
1981	8.77	7.52
1982	8.08	7.68
1983	7.83	7.72
1984	8.33	8.51
1985	7.39	8.38
1986	6.38	8.15
1987	7.02	7.89
1988	8.31	8.35
1989	8.72	7.61
1990	8.62	6.31
1991	7.69	5.52
1992	5.74	

Table 2.12. Annual Change in Labor Productivity and Unit Labor Costs (percent), United Kingdom, 1971 to 1992

Year	GDP/(Workforce in Employment)	Output per Person Employed (Whole Economy)	Output per Person Employed (Production Industries)	Unit Labor Costs (Whole Economy)	Unit Labor Costs (Manufacturing Industry)
1971	4.59	3.04	2.88	−1.19	−0.44
1972	1.82	2.39	4.28	1.07	−1.69
1973	6.24	5.21	4.47	0.26	−3.19
1974	−1.26	−1.83	−3.26	5.17	4.35
1975	−0.11	−0.40	−1.53	3.32	2.23
1976	5.15	3.47	5.44	−5.97	−4.36
1977	1.23	2.45	4.72	−6.08	−5.60
1978	2.75	2.14	1.41	−0.54	1.77
1979	1.10	1.48	4.58	−0.37	0.92
1980	−1.23	−1.33	−2.26	2.09	2.70
1981	2.78	2.34	5.84	−1.94	−2.14
1982	3.58	3.85	8.22	−2.37	−3.25
1983	4.14	4.51	9.37	−1.78	−4.80
1984	−0.28	0.33	2.17	1.31	−1.55
1985	2.98	2.76	6.16	−0.30	0.14
1986	4.07	3.76	5.10	1.31	0.71
1987	2.59	2.80	4.85	−0.45	−3.12
1988	1.73	1.21	2.72	1.11	−3.48
1989	−0.54	−0.40	0.53	2.34	−2.53
1990	0.04	−0.10	1.49	3.66	1.25
1991	1.10	0.50	3.64	1.04	0.07
1992	2.44	2.29	5.6	−0.31	−2.87

Note: Columns 1, 4, and 5 are deflated by GDP deflator.

Table 2.13. Annual Change in Labor Productivity and Unit Labor Costs (percent), United States, 1971 to 1992

Year	GNP/(Workforce in Employment)	GDP/(Workforce in Employment)	Output per Hour of All Persons (Private Business Sector)	ARC of Unit Labor Costs (Private Business Sector)	Figures of Column 4 Deflated by GNP Deflator	ARC of Unit Labor Costs (Manufacturing)
1971	2.28	2.21	3.30	3.08	−2.33	
1972	1.43	1.41	3.11	2.99	−1.88	
1973	1.77	1.53	2.59	6.03	−0.42	3.90
1974	−2.68	−2.82	−2.00	11.79	3.07	10.34
1975	0.09	0.36	2.47	7.53	−2.04	11.79
1976	1.67	1.52	2.93	5.95	−0.35	3.03
1977	0.95	0.87	1.73	6.28	−0.60	3.93
1978	0.42	0.48	0.50	8.24	0.37	6.07
1979	0.04	−0.30	−1.09	10.92	2.30	7.63
1980	−1.21	−1.17	−0.80	11.66	2.19	9.46
1981	0.47	0.65	1.32	8.00	−2.04	7.13
1982	−1.52	−1.37	0.10	7.41	1.20	4.84
1983	2.56	2.79	2.40	1.50	−2.56	−1.83
1984	1.81	2.04	2.34	1.87	−2.60	−0.39
1985	0.87	1.04	1.43	3.00	−0.62	1.67
1986	0.52	0.68	2.07	2.82	0.17	−0.58
1987	0.36	0.47	1.01	2.47	−0.73	−2.72
1988	1.82	1.76	1.00	3.39	−0.41	2.50
1989	0.62	0.47	−0.72	4.31	−0.22	2.05
1990	0.86	0.67	0.64	4.96	0.63	3.06
1991	−0.01	0.23	1.08	3.78	−0.20	3.34
1992	1.84	1.98	3.49	1.75	−1.14	0.27

Note: Columns 1 and 2 are deflated by GNP deflator and GDP deflator, respectively.

Table 2.14. Annual Change in Labor Productivity and Unit Labor Costs (percent), Japan, 1971 to 1992

Year	GNP/(Workforce in Employment)	GDP/(Workforce in Employment)	Labor Productivity Index (All Industries)	Unit Labor Cost Index (Manufacturing Industries)
1971	3.97	3.76		
1972	8.63	8.18		
1973	6.16	5.57		
1974	−0.27	−0.20	−0.24	29.77
1975	2.96	2.81	−3.68	21.98
1976	3.29	3.07	11.96	−0.23
1977	3.62	3.35	5.00	3.84
1978	3.77	3.75	8.01	−1.96
1979	4.31	4.21	11.82	−1.44
1980	2.50	2.46	8.78	2.92
1981	2.73	2.62	3.62	5.57
1982	2.07	2.13	0.48	5.90
1983	1.42	1.42	4.27	1.27
1984	3.87	3.74	9.71	−3.19
1985	4.42	4.41	4.29	1.60
1986	1.85	1.85	2.12	3.34
1987	3.30	3.31	5.71	−2.85
1988	4.53	4.61	10.57	−4.30
1989	2.91	2.86	6.33	0.00
1990	2.84	2.84	4.49	2.15
1991	2.18	2.17	2.60	3.70
1992	0.44	0.44	−4.87	9.16

Table 2.15. Annual Change in the Real Wage Rate (percent), United Kingdom, 1971 to 1992

Year	(IE + LIS)/(Workforce in Employment)	IE/(Employees in Employment)
1971	2.49	2.10
1972	5.71	5.60
1973	5.59	4.06
1974	1.23	2.88
1975	6.08	7.22
1976	−1.12	−1.91
1977	−6.38	−5.25
1978	5.09	5.24
1979	2.21	1.88
1980	2.18	1.77
1981	1.30	2.11
1982	−0.05	−0.14
1983	2.60	4.14
1984	0.57	0.93
1985	0.92	1.55
1986	6.00	4.68
1987	2.12	3.10
1988	3.68	3.00
1989	1.36	1.19
1990	1.19	−0.44
1991	1.33	2.32
1992	2.39	2.1

Table 2.16. Annual Change in the Real Wage Rate (percent), United States, 1971 to 1992

Year	IE/(Employees in Employment)	(IE + LIS)/(Workforce in Employment)
1971	2.01	1.24
1972	3.64	3.64
1973	1.36	2.89
1974	−3.49	−3.80
1975	−0.88	−1.84
1976	2.42	1.71
1977	0.84	0.42
1978	0.36	1.08
1979	−2.84	−2.13
1980	−4.34	−4.88
1981	−0.82	−1.34
1982	1.19	−0.08
1983	2.00	0.82
1984	0.68	2.06
1985	0.29	1.65
1986	2.04	2.37
1987	0.51	0.46
1988	0.82	1.19
1989	−1.31	−0.44
1990	−0.50	0.39
1991	−0.11	0.16
1992	1.59	1.98

Table 2.17. Annual Change in the Real Wage Rate (percent), Japan, 1970 to 1992

Year	IE/(Employees in Employment)	(IE + LIS)/(Workforce in Employment)
1970		
1971	6.92	7.20
1972	8.08	10.39
1973	1.57	6.35
1974	−0.62	5.22
1975	2.92	4.27
1976	1.14	2.22
1977	1.06	−0.15
1978	3.03	2.16
1979	1.98	2.40
1980	−2.15	−3.73
1981	1.22	0.79
1982	1.57	1.61
1983	1.89	1.46
1984	1.60	1.45
1985	1.47	2.76
1986	2.80	2.64
1987	2.43	2.56
1988	2.63	2.80
1989	1.70	2.32
1990	1.79	2.36
1991	0.93	1.66
1992		

NOTES

1. See Appendix 2A for a discussion of the labor and asset bases and the validity of the estimates for Japan and the United Kingdom, respectively.
2. See Appendix 2A to this chapter.
3. LIS is calculated by the following:

United Kingdom: Income from self-employment (IS) – (Gross trading profit (GTP)) × (Net capital stock ratio of unincorporated to incorporated Enterprises (NCSR)).
United States: IS (Proprietor's Income) – PI (Corporate Profits) × NCSR.
Japan: IS – (Profits of incorporated enterprises) × (Gross capital stock ratio of unincorporated to incorporated enterprises (GCSR)).

4. Our productivity equations and some supplementary calculations are in line with conventional measures. There are some discussions on these.

Spencer (1987 and 1988), for example, argues as follows: The most commonly used measures of labor productivity are output per head and output per hour; however, these measures of labor input are unsatisfactory in many ways. In particular, they make no allowance for changes in labor utilization or for the pace at which the workforce operates. Then he takes a sophisticated method that has been pioneered by Muellbauer (1986). The method derives an explicit measure of labor utilization based on overtime hours, which has the effect of removing cyclical variations and leaves a relatively smooth measure of productivity (Spencer, 1988, pp. 2–3).

This method has the advantage of showing the underlying trend of productivity in the long run. However, there are also disadvantages: first, the factor utilization varies with the level of demand; as Spencer says that "in practice capital goods are not homogeneous but are designed for particular manning levels, which are often rather inflexible" (1987, p. 12) in the short run.

Therefore, an adjustment in the first stage to the change of demand is made by using overtime hours or short-time working subject to the employment contract. The next stage of coping with the slackened demand is a labor deduction, which affects manning levels. This will be made disproportionately between the direct (manual) and the overhead (nonmanual) labor, and this in turn has a strong effect on labor productivity. We consider this point important.

Second, it is difficult to have utilization-adjusted labor productivity in the nonmanufacturing industry. As Spencer suggests, this is partly because service-sector output is difficult to estimate, due to its nonphysical nature. In addition, labor data outside manufacturing are poor.

For these reasons, I consider that an averaged growth rate in productivity based on the customary measure could be the second-best alternative for measuring the growth trend in the long run.

5. See Appendix 2B.
6. GDP data for adjustment are as follows. We show their incidence only around the years in question.

The United Kingdom: The annual growth rates as percentages of GDP at a constant price for the years 1983 to 1986 are 3.9, 2.0, 4.2, and 4.4, respectively. The business cycle in the middle 1980s is weak. A trough year is 1971, as is indicated by the cyclical indicator. However, the real GDP growth rates calculated by the *Datastream* data for the years 1971 to 1972 are 3.1 percent and 2.6 percent, respectively.

The United States: The real annual growth rates as percentages of GDP are 1988 (4.1), 1989 (2.6), 1990 (1.2), 1991 (−0.7), and 1992 (2.6). The growth rates were negative in trough years in the United States.

Japan: The real annual growth rates of GDP for the years 1982 to 1984 are 3.4 percent, 2.8 percent, and 4.3 percent, respectively.

The annual growth rates of GNP in real terms in the above years are also similar to those of GDP in each country.

7. As we mentioned in a preceding note, the business cycle in the middle 1980s in the United Kingdom was weak. This is also demonstrated by the coincident indicators (the difference in

index between the peak and the trough was 5.40, but in the adjusted case only 2.78). (See Matthews and Minford (1987) for an explanation of the strong government policies by which the economy was affected in these years.)

In the case of Japan, the business recession in 1977 was also weak, and the recession period was nine months (peak to trough was from Q1 to Q4 in 1977). We adjusted trough and peak years for GDP (and GNP), but GDP growth rates for the years 1976 and 1977 were 4.61 percent and 5.12 percent, respectively. The diffusion index for 1977 was 47.7. For industries (manufacturing, production, and so on), considering this weak cycle may be important (for the business cycle relates closely to industries).

8. See Appendix 2C to this chapter. The figures in the text correspond to the tables in the appendix.

9. According to the earlier work for the United Kingdom (Iyoda, 1985), the labor share estimated on the labor basis moved countercyclically during the period 1961 to 1980, but for 1951 to 1960 and 1980 to 1982 the movements were somewhat procyclical.

A symmetrical change in the labor share based on the labor basis was perfect for the years 1955 to 1982, which covered five business cycles. On the asset basis, it had only two exceptions (1969 and 1973) for the years 1952 to 1982, which covered six business cycles (Iyoda, 1985, table 1 and fig. 1).

10. A fairly good countercyclical movement of the Japanese labor share has been observed by Iyoda (1987) for the years 1950 to 1985. It was clearer in the revised estimate based on the asset basis for 1970 to 1985, taking into consideration stock valuation adjustment and statistical discrepancies. A simple method of incorporating denominators into the labor share estimate was used adding stock valuation adjustment and deducting statistical discrepancies. Because around the years in question related to trough and peak, these volumes in particular stock valuation adjustment are relatively large (Iyoda, 1987, table 2).

Taking trough and peak years on a yearly base, the countercyclical movements were perfect during the period 1955 to 1985, which covered six business cycles. The labor share increased in the trough years and decreased in the peak years. In the revised estimate, years 1973 and 1976 follow on countercyclical movements. These years are not exceptions.

An estimate of the exempted years 1950 to 1954 might possibly have been affected by the following facts: data during these period are less reliable than for other years of observation, and the capital stock estimate depends on my own (Iyoda, 1987, figs. 2 and 3).

11. Taking a revised estimate into consideration, the symmetrical change in the labor share is very clear during the period 1955 to 1985; there is only one exception—1975 (Iyoda, 1987, figs. 2 and 3).

12. Some facts show this structural change. The percentage of income from employment in national income showed a sharp increase from 54.0 (1970) to 67.5 (1975). In contrast, during the same years, the percentage of incorporated profits sharply decreased from 37.7 to 21.6, and to a lesser extent self-employed income from 17.1 to 14.1 followed the same pattern (EPA, *ANA*, (1993), pt. 2, [2]IV, 2; for *ANA*, see Appendix 2B). The gross domestic fixed capital formation decreased from 35.5 (1970) to 31.1 (1975) in terms of percentage distribution of GNP (EPA, *ANA*, (1993), pt. 2, [2]IV, 1).

13. Japan continued to have an averaged rate of (about) 10 percent annual growth for nearly two decades after 1955.

14. On a macroeconomy level, under a high rate of inflation, stock valuation relates to profits (refer to note 10 regarding the relative share of labor). However, on a microeconomy level, the high rate of inflation has far larger possibility affecting profits: capital gains, debtor's benefit (profit), and underdepreciation caused by the historical cost (book value) rule all relate to the volume of profits.

15. This will be partly explained by a consideration of the difference of their productivity growth. An averaged growth rate in manufacturing in terms of output per person employed was 3.26 percent during the period from 1971 to 1992. However, the same kind of productivity

growth in the production industry (which includes manufacturing) was 3.56 percent (higher by 0.3 percent point than manufacturing) during the same period (CSO, *ET* (1993), T23; Department of Employment, *EG* (September 1993), T1.8).

16. Net operating profits, whose rate fairly corresponds to the phase in the business cycle, are not figures in the national income but are collected from incorporated businesses (with share capital of 10 million Yen and above). The profit rate based on the national income base has not always a good fit. Despite the fact that private corporations recorded one of the highest periods of ordinary profits in the latter half of fiscal year 1973, the labor share was in increasing trend from 1970 to 1976.

This is explained as the monetary illusion that was caused by the differences between the national income base and the corporate accounting principles in Japan. Economic Planning Agency (1977, ch. IV, sec. 2) gives us an effective hint at the explanation.

The corporate profits based on the national income base are the net product of corporations less the costs of wages, salaries, and finance, aiming at calculating the economic activity taken as a whole. The depreciation is estimated at the current prices of capital goods, but the capital gain does not consist of the net product for the year, considering that profits accrued from inflation are a kind of transfer income. On the other hand, based on the corporate accounting principles, the depreciation is estimated at the book values of capital goods, and the profit accrued from inventory valuation consists of corporate profits as ordinary profit at the time of its realization, and debtor's profit accrued from inflation as extraordinary profit (Iyoda, 1979, p. 28; 1980b, pp. 668–669).

17. For example, the output growth rates in the manufacturing in percentage terms are 2.85 (1983), 3.84 (1984), 2.67 (1985), *1.30 (1986)*, 5.23 (1987), 7.04 (1988), *4.29 (1989)*, and −0.50 (1990), respectively.

The weight of manufacturing product in GDP at factor cost is at most one-quarter, and this has been decreasing (around 22 to 23 percent in recent years since 1991 to 1992) (CSO, *ETAS* (1993), calculated from T15; for *ETAS*, see Appendix 2B).

18. See notes 6 and 7 for a discussion of the weak cycle.

19. During the years 1972 to 1974, the percentage share of self-employment income in the net national product increased, despite its long-term tendency to decrease, during the years 1972 to 1974 (16.2, 17.7, 17.2), respectively. Similar increases were also observed in the United Kingdom during those periods. The percentages of self-employed income in GNP were 8.9 (1970), 9.9 (1971), 10.8 (1972), and 9.9 (1973) (Iyoda, 1984, table 3.)

20. See the rate of profit of incorporated enterprises in Figure 2.7.

21. Proprietors' incomes with inventory valuation and capital consumption adjustments from 1980 to 1983 were 171.8, 180.8, 170.7, and 186.7 (billions of dollars), respectively. In contrast, compensation of employees from 1980 to 1983 were 1644.5, 1815.5, 1916.0, and 2029.4, respectively (billions of dollars) (Council of Economic Advisers, *ERP* (1992), table 22; for this source, see Appendix 2B).

22. See Appendix 2A for an explanation of these different movements.

23. See note 10 of this chapter. Year 1973 is not an exception in the revised estimate.

24. Refer to note 10 of this Chapter.

25. We might add a possibility of some biased results due to the nature of the data used. For example, data on the United States labor force are not strictly comparable with earlier data because of population adjustments (1972, 1973, 1978, and 1986); U.S. total employees were calculated by using different series data. There may be some biased results. However, we consider that the degree of bias would not be large enough to distort the fact greatly.

26. Dore (1993, pp. 19–21) presents ten stylized facts for twentieth-century business cycles, especially those observed in market economies after World War II. His stylized facts regarding productivity and profits mostly correspond with our stylized facts: "(6) a procyclical relationship between productivity and output" and "(7) the general procyclical nature of profits." However, his stylized fact, regarding the real wages is arguable: "(3) procyclical real wages indicating that the wage share out of national income is also procyclical."

Our observation is limited to three countries and twenty-two years. Furthermore, our calculation equations for the real wage rate are

$$\frac{\text{IE (Income from employment)}}{\text{Employees}},$$

and

$$\frac{\text{IE + LIS (Labor income from self-employment)}}{\text{Labor force employed}},$$

both of which are deflated by the consumer price index (or the retail price index) (see the section on Equations for Calculation for details).

Real wages are procyclical in the United States (Figure 2.12). However, for the United Kingdom, it is hard to believe procyclical real wages (Figure 2.11). For Japan, the results are in between the United States and the United Kingdom. The estimate calculated by

$$\frac{\text{IE}}{\text{Employees}}$$

is more similar to that of United States, but the growth rate is stable in the 1980s (Figure 2.13). For further details, refer to The Real Wage Rate in this chapter and Table 2.3.

Our observation years are limited, so it may be useful to mention about a different observation calculated by the same formula for Japan. Iyoda (1980a, p. 8, table 2; 1980b, p. 676, fig. 3) shows that the year-to-year difference of the real wage growth was not so great except during the recession triggered by the oil shock of 1973. The growth rate does not always show an outstanding decrease even in a slump (even an increase observed in a slump year of 1958), with its growth rate amounting to a great average of 6.3 percent during the period between 1955 and 1976. We observe, as a whole, fairly weak procyclical real wages during the period for Japan in terms of growth rate.

Dore presents a number of large studies that support procyclical real wages: Dunlop (1938), Tarshis (1939), Bodkin (1969), Bils (1985), Raisian (1983), and Keane, Moffitt, and Runkle (1988). He also presents theoretical studies of Barro and Grossman (1971) that relate to this question. A few studies supporting countercyclical real wages that he presents are Neftci (1978) and Sargent (1978). However, these two studies are claimed by Gearly and Kennan (1982) (refer to Dore, 1993, pp. 24–25).

Greenwald and Stiglitz (1988) establish the facts for reviewing the ability of the new classical, traditional Keynesian, and new Keynesian theories. In relation to our research, their established facts are that employment, hours, and productivity move procyclically but unemployment moves countercyclically. Variations in real wages are at best weakly procyclical. The real wages move differently depending on the deflator used. When producer prices are used, wages are weakly countercyclical in the United States and Australia. When the consumer price index is used, they are procyclical except for Australia. The countries sampled are the United States, Japan, West Germany, the United Kingdom, and Australia. The degree of fluctuation varies from country to country and from observation periods (pp. 223–234). These facts are mostly the same as those of Dore. However, the nuance is slightly different for real wages.

27. King and Regan (1976, p. 17) say that "rare unanimity prevails with respect to cyclical movements in income shares."

Solow (1966, p. 454) presents models in the short run as well as long run. He quotes the studies of Kuh (1960, 1963) and Neild (1963) that:

Kuh has found for the United States (confirmed by Neild's findings for Britain) that, in the course of these fluctuations in output and employment, the ratio of p/w of prices to money wages is much more stable (apart from trend) than the ratio Q/L of real output per manhour [in manufacturing industries]. Since the product of these two ratios is the reciprocal of the wage share, this amounts to saying that short-run changes in distributions are primarily a reflection of short-run changes in productivity.

Expressing this by our above identity (2.1), the ratio ω_m/e is much more stable (apart from trend) than μ. Therefore, short-run changes in ρ_1 are primarily a reflection of short-run changes in productivity.

Solow (1966, p. 456) mentions the difficulty of the short-run production function in this explanation. If the short-run production function is assumed to be of the normal shape with constant returns to scale and diminishing returns as the capital/output ratio varies, actual procyclical change of productivity will not be explained. To explain this procyclical productivity change, Solow presents a short-run model of labor hoarding, which is based on the assumption of a typical firm under oligopoly and on cost-minimization (pp. 457–462). He emphasizes that "a pattern of productivity behaviour . . . can be produced as the result of entirely rational cost-minimization without invoking sharply-falling unit costs" (p. 461). When we restrict our attention only to a pattern of productivity behavior, this is perhaps one of the possible model to explain it.

However, when we intend to deal with the whole economy, which includes manufacturing industries, Solow's restricted approach will decrease its interpretative value. Iyoda (1980a, table 3; 1980b, fig. 2-a) estimated the relative influences of ω_m, e, and μ on the change of ρ_1 by the above equation (2.2) on a whole economy, during the years from 1955 to 1976 for Japan, taking the GNP deflator as e. These influences were expressed in percentage distributions of the degree of contribution that were measured as percentages of the degree of contribution by each factor per sum of each degree of contribution in terms of absolute value.

The percentage distributions of ω_m, e, and μ were on average 49.2, 23.1, and 27.1, respectively. Restricting to five trough years during the observation period, these respective values averaged 57.5, 20.6, and 21.9. According to this result for Japan, the influence of money wage rate is fairly large, even if deducting price percentages from money wages percentages, the differences (in terms of percentage points) are still great enough and vary from 7.6 to 46.0 compared with productivity percentages from 2.0 to 47.0. In this case productivity is not a sole important factor in explaining short-run changes in distributions.

28. For the U.S. economy, see Hahnell and Sherman (1982). They explain this phenomenon by "wage lag" and "overhead labour" theses (refer to Hahnell and Sherman for a more detailed explanation).

29. One might add a third method, *the proportional basis*. This method divides income from self-employment between labor and property in the same ratio as it is distributed in incorporated enterprises or applies some other arbitrary ratio. However, this is not affected by particular situations in self-employed businesses that are different from incorporated enterprises—the ratio of male- to all-self-employed persons, their average age, a structural change of self-employed businesses in the long run, the existence of family workers, and so on. So I consider this method not reliable. (For an explanation of these measures, see King and Regan, 1976, pp. 13–14.)

30. Feldstein and Summers (1977, pp. 212–213) discuss these points.

31. Our data for estimation are yearly, so there is no relation to seasonal adjustment. However, the same *Datastream* code is used between yearly data and quarterly data (if applicable); it has symbols relating to this seasonal adjustment.

32. PBT is not comparable with the old series before 1973. We adjusted the profit rate estimate (for the years 1970–73) for the following formula:

$$\frac{\text{Profit Rate 1973IV (New)}}{\text{Profit Rate 1973IV (Old)}} \times \text{Data (Old, each year)}.$$

3. KALDOR'S MODEL

Kaldor presented his remarkable paper "Alternative Theories of Distribution" in the *Review of Economic Studies* (1955–1956). The theory of income distribution has been the principal problem in political economy since Ricardo, and Kaldor presented a bird's-eye view of the various theoretical attempts since Ricardo at solving this problem. He took up Ricardian or classical theory, Marxian, neoclassical or marginalist theory, and Keynesian as four main strands of thought. His "Keynesian theory," now called "Kaldor's model," is characterized as an application of Keynesian principle of the multiplier and of the idea of widow's cruse.

On the theory of income distribution, Kaldor (1955–1956, p. 210) says that

> In fact no hypothesis as regards the forces determining distributive shares could be intellectually satisfying unless it succeeded in accounting for the relative stability of these shares in the advanced capitalist economies over the last 100 years or so, despite the phenomenal changes in the technique of production, in the accumulation of capital relative to labour and in real income per head.

However, how successful will his model be in explaining the distribution of income in the actual economy?

In this chapter, Kaldor's original model of income distribution is presented and then interpreted by using some additional forms. His model is discussed by referring to various comments on it and his recognition of historical constancies. Finally, an assessment of his model shows a weakness when applied to an underemployment economy.

KALDOR'S MODEL

A Model

Kaldor begins by assuming a state of full employment (and later shows the conditions under which a state of full employment will result from his model). Under full employment, total output or income Y is given, which may be divided into two broad categories, wages W and profits P.

Writing S_w and S_p, for aggregate savings S out of wages and profits, he has the following income identities:

$$Y \equiv W + P$$

$$I \equiv S$$

$$S \equiv S_w + S_p.$$

Taking investment I as given, and assuming simple proportional savings $S_w = s_w W$ and $S_p = s_p P$, he obtains

$$I = s_p P + s_w W = s_p P + s_w(Y - P) = (s_p - s_w)P + s_w Y,$$

which results in

$$\frac{I}{Y} = (s_p - s_w)\frac{P}{Y} + s_w \tag{1}$$

and

$$\frac{P}{Y} = \frac{1}{s_p - s_w} \cdot \frac{I}{Y} - \frac{s_w}{s_p - s_w} \tag{2}$$

Thus, given the wage earners' s_w and the capitalists' s_p propensities to save, the share of profits in income P/Y depends simply on the ratio of investment to output I/Y.

According to Kaldor, the interpretative value of the model (as distinct from the formal validity of the equations, or identities), as he emphasizes, depends on the Keynesian hypothesis that investment, or rather the ratio of investment to output, can be treated as an independent variable, invariant with respect to changes in the two savings propensities s_p and s_w.[1]

The model operates only if

$s_p \neq s_w$, and

$s_p > s_w$.

The latter is a stability condition. The degree of stability of the system depends on the difference of the marginal propensities—that is, on $1/(s_p - s_w)$, which may be termed the *coefficient of sensitivity of income distribution.*

The critical assumption is that the investment/output ratio is an independent variable. Following Harrod, he describes the determinants of the investment/output ratio in terms of the rate of growth of output capacity G and the capital/output ratio v:

$$\frac{I}{Y} = Gv. \tag{3}$$

In a state of continuous full employment, G must be equal to the rate of growth of the *full-employment ceiling* G'—namely, the sum of the rate of technical progress and the growth in working population (Harrod's natural rate of growth). For Harrod's second equation,[2]

$$\frac{I}{Y} = s,$$

where $s = S/Y$,

he substitutes equation (1) above:

$$\frac{I}{Y}(= s) = (s_p - s_w)\frac{P}{Y} + s_w.$$

Hence the *warranted* and the *natural* rates of growth are not independent of one another; if profit margins are flexible, the former will adjust itself to the latter through a consequential change in P/Y.[3] The model, he emphasizes, shows the share of profits P/Y, the rate of profit on capital P/vY, and the real wage rate W/L, as functions of I/Y, which in turn is determined independently of P/Y or W/L.

Restraint Conditions to the Model

Kaldor presents the following four conditions as restraints.

1. The real wage cannot fall below a certain subsistence minimum. Hence P/Y can attain its indicated value only if the resulting real wage exceeds this minimum rate w'. The model is subject to the restriction

$$\frac{P}{Y} \leq \frac{Y - w'L}{Y}. \tag{4}$$

2. The indicated share of profits cannot be below the level that yields the minimum rate of profit necessary to induce capitalists to invest their capital and that he calls the risk *premium rate* r'. Hence the restriction

$$\frac{P}{vY} \geq r'. \tag{5}$$

3. There may be a certain minimum rate of profit on turnovers and so on, which he calls m, the *degree of monopoly* rate. Hence the restriction

$$\frac{P}{Y} \geq m. \tag{6}$$

Equations (5) and (6) describe alternative restriction, of which the higher will apply.

4. The capital/output ratio v should not in itself be influenced by the rate of profit, for if it is, the investment/output ratio Gv will itself be dependent on the rate of profit. To exclude this he assumes that v is invariant to P/Y—that is,

$$v = \bar{v}. \tag{7}$$

According to Kaldor, if equations (2) to (6) are all satisfied, there will be an inherent tendency to growth and an inherent tendency to full employment. This is a possible interpretation of the long-term situation in the capitalist economies of Western Europe and North America. However, several reasons can be adduced to show why the system will not be flexible enough to ensure full employment in the short period: (1) a limited mobility of resources between the consumption goods and the investment goods industries and (2) the downward inflexibility of P/Y and the downward inflexibility of W/L. Hence in the short period the shares of profits and wages tend to be inflexible for the downward inflexibility of both P/Y and W/L, which thus tend to reinforce the long-period stability of these shares, due to constancy of I/Y, resulting from the long-period constancy of Gv and $G'v$.

INTERPRETATION

This section attempts to interpret Kaldor's model under full employment by using additional identities, further clarifying what the model explains. The economy considered is one in which both capital and labor force are fully employed.

Reformulation of the Model[4]

Some additional notations are used in the following explanation.

K = capital stock	K_v = value of capital stock
e = price level	μ = labor productivity (Y/eL)
ω = real wage rate	ω_m = money wage rate
π = profit rate	

The share of profits in income was determined by equation (2):

$$\frac{P}{Y} = \frac{I}{Y(s_p - s_w)} - \frac{s_w}{s_p - s_w}. \tag{2}$$

Then, we have

$$\rho_c = \frac{C - s_w}{s_p - s_w}, \tag{2-1}$$

where

$\rho_c = P/Y$,

$C = I/Y$, and

$C > s_w$.[5]

The capital/output ratio identity is expressed by

$$v \equiv K_v/Y.$$

Considering that $K_v \equiv eK$ and $Y \equiv e\mu L$, we have

$$\begin{aligned} v &= eK/e\mu L \\ &= k/\mu \end{aligned} \tag{a}$$

where

$k = K/L$.

The profit rate and the real wage rate are expressed by the following identity, respectively:

$$\begin{aligned} \pi &\equiv \frac{P}{Y} \cdot \frac{Y}{K_v} \\ &= \rho_c/v. \end{aligned} \tag{b}$$

$$\omega \equiv \frac{\omega_m}{e} = \frac{W}{eL},$$

where

$$W = \omega_m L,^6$$

from which we have

$$\begin{aligned}\omega &= \frac{Y}{eL}\left(\frac{W}{Y}\right) \\ &= \frac{e\mu L}{eL}\left(1 - \frac{P}{Y}\right) \\ &= \mu(1 - \rho_c). \qquad \text{(c)}\end{aligned}$$

Finally, the price level derives from the real wage rate identity above:

$$e = \frac{\omega_m}{\omega}. \qquad \text{(d)}$$

By equations (2-1), (a), (b), (c), and (d), it is possible for us to draw some conclusions from Kaldor's model:

1. According to Keynesian hypothesis, the investment/output ratio is treated as an independent variable, which plays a strategic role in determining the distributive shares of income.
2. The real wage rate, the relative share of property, the profit rate, and the price level are not independent from two savings propensities, s_p and s_w.
3. The profit rate π depends on the methods of measuring capital K_v. If K_v is measured by replacement cost, π is determined independently from the price level e. But when it is measured by the historical cost (the purchased value), π will vary with the price level.[7]
4. In contrast to Ricardian (classical school), it is not profits but wages that are determined as a residual.

Further Interpretation

For a further interpretation, consider a respective growth rate form from (2-1), (a), (b), (c), and (d).

From (2-1), we have

$$\hat{\rho}_c = \frac{\dot{C} - \dot{s}_w}{C - s_w} - \frac{\dot{s}_p - \dot{s}_w}{s_p - s_w}. \qquad \text{(2-1')}$$

We have a growth rate form of v from equation (a):

$$\hat{v} = \hat{k} - \hat{\mu}. \tag{a'}$$

From (b), we have

$$\hat{\pi} = \hat{\rho}_c - \hat{v}. \tag{b'}$$

Using (a′) and (b′), we have

$$\hat{\pi} = \hat{\rho}_c - (\hat{k} - \hat{\mu}). \tag{b''}$$

We have a growth rate form of the real wage rate from (c):

$$\hat{\omega} = \hat{\mu} - \frac{\dot{\rho}_c}{1 - \rho_c}. \tag{c'}$$

Finally, we have a growth rate form of the price level from (d):

$$\hat{e} = \hat{\omega}_m - \hat{\omega}. \tag{d'}$$

Using (c′) and (d′), we have

$$\hat{e} = \hat{\omega}_m - \left(\hat{\mu} - \frac{\dot{\rho}_c}{1 - \rho_c}\right). \tag{d''}$$

In the Short Run

Under full employment in the short run, suppose that savings propensities out of wages and profits (s_w and s_p), the capital/output ratio v, and the labor productivity μ are constants.

In this case, growth rate forms (2-1′), (a′), (b″), (c′), and (d″) become the following, respectively:

$$\hat{\rho}_c = \frac{\dot{C}}{C - s_w} \tag{2-1''}$$

$$\hat{k} = 0 \tag{a''}$$

$$\hat{\pi} = \hat{\rho}_c \tag{b''-1}$$

$$\hat{\omega} = -\frac{\dot{\rho}_c}{1 - \rho_c} \tag{c''}$$

$$\hat{e} = \hat{\omega}_m + \frac{\dot{\rho}_c}{1 - \rho_c}. \tag{d''-1}$$

Suppose that the investment/output ratio increases to above the level that sustains full employment. Then, it turns out that the relative share of profits ρ_c will increase from equation (2-1″). By equation (b″-1) the profit rate will also increase because of $\hat{\rho}_c > 0$. However the real wage rate will decrease from equation (c″). Assuming nonnegative growth of the money wage rate, it turns out, from this (d″-1) form, that our economy faces a possibility of an increase in the share of profits leading to an increase of the money wage rate, which in turn results in the high rate of price increase.

In the Long Run

Consider a full-employment economy in the long run where s_p, s_w, v, and μ are no longer constants. However, suppose that s_w and s_p are constants for simplicity in equation (2-1) and that the investment/output ratio is

$$C \geq C_f.$$

Here C_f denotes the investment/output ratio that sustains full employment. Changes in the profit rate, the real wage rate, and the price leavel are explained in the following.

CASE I. $\dot{C} \geq 0$. When the investment/output ratio increases,[8] the profit share will increase from (2-1″) ($\hat{\rho}_c \geq 0$). In this case, the following relationship is derived from (b″), (c′), and (d″), respectively:

$$\hat{\rho}_c \gtreqless \hat{k} - \hat{\mu} \quad \Rightarrow \quad \hat{\pi} \gtreqless 0, \tag{i}$$

$$\hat{\mu} \gtreqless \frac{\dot{\rho}_c}{1 - \rho_c} \quad \Rightarrow \quad \hat{\omega} \gtreqless 0, \tag{ii}$$

and when $\hat{\omega}_m \geq 0$,

$$\hat{\omega}_m \gtreqless \hat{\mu} - \frac{\dot{\rho}_c}{1 - \rho_c} \quad \Rightarrow \quad \hat{e} \gtreqless 0. \tag{iii}$$

CASE II. $\dot{C} < 0$. When the investment/output ratio decreases but is larger than the minimum level to sustain the full employment economy, the profit share will decrease from (2-1″) ($\hat{\rho}_c < 0$). We similarly have the following relationship.

Concerning the profit rate, from (b″)

When $\hat{k} - \hat{\mu} \geq 0$, then $\hat{\pi} \leq 0$, and (ia)

when $\hat{k} - \hat{\mu} < 0$, then

$$|\hat{\rho}_c| \lesseqgtr |\hat{k} - \hat{\mu}| \quad \Rightarrow \quad \hat{\pi} \gtreqless 0. \tag{ib}$$

We have changes of the real wage rate from (c′):

When $\hat{\mu} \geq 0$, then $\hat{\omega} > 0$, and (iia)

when $\hat{\mu} < 0$, then

$$|\hat{\mu}| \underset{>}{\overset{<}{=}} \left|\frac{\dot{\rho}_c}{1-\rho_c}\right| \quad \Rightarrow \quad \hat{\omega} \underset{<}{\overset{>}{=}} 0. \tag{iib}$$

Concerning the price level, from (d″)

When $\hat{\omega}_m > 0$, then

$$\hat{\omega}_m \underset{<}{\overset{>}{=}} \hat{\mu} - \frac{\dot{\rho}_c}{1-\rho_c} \quad \Rightarrow \quad \hat{e} \underset{<}{\overset{>}{=}} 0. \tag{iiia}$$

We explained the logical relationship in the long run but did not consider equilibrium values in the long run because, as was observed in Chapter 2, there is no equilibrium value over the period of a couple of decades.[9]

Therefore we dealt with Kaldor's model under dynamic movement, but still sustaining a full-employment economy. However, if we look at various cases, variable μ (labor productivity) is included in each condition. Productivity growth is a matter of fact but makes an important role in determining the changes of π, ω, and e. Per capita capital growth $\hat{k}$ and per capita investment growth $\hat{\imath}_r$ (see note 8) are also important. A growth theory is needed for further discussion.

To explain fully changes of ρ, π, ω, and e in the long run, a growth theory is needed that incorporates technological changes into the theory. Later on Kaldor developed his growth model and his unique technical production function. However, this is beyond the discussion here.[10]

COMMENTS

The model was a sensational presentation. Various and some critical comments were made from the neoclassical school in relation to the marginal approach and from Keynesians as well. It aroused a polemic between Cambridge, United Kingdom, and Cambridge, Massachusetts (MIT and Harvard) economists in the 1960s.[11] Among the U.K. Cambridge economists, an attempt by Pasinetti (1962) was made to revise and develop Kaldor's model.

This book neither traces the polemic nor deals with the discussions presented there in detail, but I demonstrate in Chapter 4 my understanding of and perspective on some of the important questions for theoretical development.

Pasinetti's Question

Pasinetti's criticism relates to Kaldor's sets in the model using two broad classes —capitalists and workers. If the workers' propensity to save is positive, workers also have capital and gain profits. Taking this factor into consideration, he revised Kaldor's model and dealt with the related matter.

The difference between Kaldor and Pasinetti stems from their different treatment of s_p and s_w. Kaldor divides income into two broad categories, wages and profits, and regards s_p and s_w as the propensity to save of capitalists and wage-earners, respectively. Pasinetti further divides profits into two parts between those that accrue to the capitalists and those that accrue to the workers. As Samuelson and Modigliani (1966a, p. 270) point out, for example, Kaldor's treatment of two broad class categories still holds true if s_p and s_w are regarded as the propensity to save of profits and wages, respectively. Or it might be possible to assume the sum of wages and salaries earned by the capitalists is equivalent to that of the profits gained by the workers.[12] For capitalists are also working to some extent and earn labor income.

Pasinetti's discussion is based on an assumption of the dynamic equilibrium condition (1962, p. 271),

$$\frac{K_w}{K} = \frac{S_w}{S},$$

but these special assumptions will not be normally satisfied. Here K_w and S_w denote capital and savings of workers, respectively. Robinson (1966, p. 308) criticizes this golden age approach by saying that "it would be better to say that a golden age is a logical construction without history, in which there is no distinction between the future and the past."

Capital Coefficient, *v*

If the capital/output ratio v is influenced by the profit rate, the investment/output ratio Gv will itself be dependent on the rate of profit. Then Kaldor's equation (2) is not applicable. To exclude this he assumes that v is invariant to P/Y.

This is one of the points dividing Kaldor and the neoclassicals. Kaldor (1955–1956, p. 234 n. 2) says that "This assumption does not necessarily mean that there are 'fixed coefficients' as between capital equipment and labour—only that technical innovations (which are also assumed 'neutral' in their effects) are far more influential on the chosen v than price relationships."

The writer basically agrees with this Kaldor's treatment. The sensitiveness of v to P/Y will not be so high if the following facts are considered: once capital is invested, the technical coefficient between capital equipment and labor becomes more or less fixed until the capital equipment is renewed. Therefore, the change of P/Y should not be temporary in order that v can be sensitive to it. It is required for this that, in the case of a rise of P/Y, for example, entrepreneurs have the prospect that either the level of P/Y will be maintained or the rise will continue. Even if there is a certain amount of marginal change in v in accordance with the change of P/Y, the change of v on average may not be so large, unless the marginal change of v continues towards the same direction for a fairly long period.

An Assumption of the Full Employment

There is a criticism about the full-employment assumption. Kaldor seeks the determinant of the distributive shares by investment-savings equilibrium on the demand side but neglects or pays scant attention to the supply side. His full-employment assumption makes this treatment possible.[13]

Kaldor's aim was to build a model that would explain the relative stability of the distributive shares in the advanced capitalist economies. Hence we consider his model based on the full-employment assumption in the long run. He (1955–1956, p. 234) says that "If equations (5) and (6) are unsatisfied, the full employment breaks down." We understand these (5) and (6) are the supply-side conditions by which entrepreneurs decide the levels of investment sufficient to sustain full employment.

However, economies are not exempt from economic fluctuations in the short run, and underemployment situations are very often observed. In this case, I/Y will not be given because Y is not given in the model. Even if investment I is given, the relative share of property ρ_c can not be determined only by equation (2). If the output Y is not given, then we have two unknown variables (Y, P) in equation (2). Kaldor's model cannot explain these situations, for it lacks an equation that determines the volume of employment (then the volume of output) in an underemployment economy. In this respect, his model is incomplete.

In reply to this equation, some Keynesians, as stated earlier in Chapter 1, introduced the first postulate of the classical theory of employment and completed the model.[14] They call it a *general model of income distribution*. Rather than express it in this way, I presents alternative models from different viewpoints in Chapter 4.

HISTORICAL CONSTANCIES

Kaldor's Recognition

In the beginning of this chapter, we quoted from Kaldor (1955–1956, p. 210) that "no hypothesis as regards the forces determining distributive shares could be intellectually satisfying in accounting for the relative stability of these shares over the last 100 years or so." He recognizes the historical constancy of the distributive shares and considers that a model should be constructed to account for these.

Kaldor (1957a, p. 270) says that "A satisfactory model concerning the nature of the growth process in a capitalist economy must also account for the remarkable historical constancies revealed by recent empirical investigations." He presents the following three as historical constancies:[15]

- The share of wages and the share of profits in the national income have shown a remarkable constancy in the developed capitalist economies of the United States and the United Kingdom since the second half of the nineteenth century.
- The value of the capital equipment per worker (measured at constant prices) and the value of the annual output per worker (also in constant prices) are steadily rising, but the trend rate of increase of both of these factors has tended to be the same, so as to leave the capital/output ratio virtually unchanged over longer periods.
- Constancy in the share of profit and in the capital/output ratio also involves constancy in the rate of profit earned on investment (in the *marginal efficiency* of capital) and this again appears to be confirmed by empirical investigations.

Kaldor (1957b) presents a simple model of economic growth.[16] In the model he introduces a unique technical progress function that shows the rate of growth of labor productivity (and income) as an increasing function of the rate of net investment expressed as a proportion of the stock of capital:

$$\frac{Y_{t+1} - Y_t}{Y_t} = \alpha'' + \beta'' \frac{I_t}{K_t},$$

where $\alpha'' > 0$ and $1 > \beta'' > 0$.

Later on, regarding the process of economic change and development in capitalist societies, Kaldor (1961) suggests the following six stylized facts that include the above three historical constancies as a starting point for the construction of theoretical models:[17]

- The continued growth in the aggregate volume of production and in the productivity of labor at a steady trend rate;
- A continued increase in the amount of capital per worker, whatever statistical measure of capital is chosen in this connection;
- A steady rate of profit on capital, at least in the developed capitalist societies (this rate of profit being substantially higher than the pure long-term rate of interest as shown by the yield of gilt-edged bonds);
- Steady capital/output ratios over long-term trends (at least no clear long-term trends, either rising or falling, if differences in the degree of utilization of capacity are allowed for);
- A high correlation between the share of profits in income and the share of investment in output (a steady share of profits (and of wages) in societies and/or in periods in which the investment coefficient (the share of investment in output) is constant); and
- Appreciable differences in the rate of growth of labor productivity and of total output in different societies, the range of variation being of the order of 2 to 5 percent.

However, the above propositions concerning the constancy of relative shares and of the capital/output ratio are applicable to countries with differing rates of growth.

Arguments on the Historical Constancies

Kaldor quotes Brown and Hart (1952) to show the stability of relative shares of *wages* in national income for the United Kingdom. However, when we calculate the relative share of *wages and salaries* in national income from the same table (Brown and Hart (1952), pp. 276–277, table 1) it is not stable, being fairly higher after World War I.[18] Kuznets (1966, table 4.2) shows that the relative share of labor in the national income has risen since after World War I for the United Kingdom and after World War II for the United States. Kravis (1959) also shows that the relative share of labor in the national income rose after World War I for the United States.

Lutz (1961, pp. x–xi) summarizes the discussion on the question of the stability of the capital/output ratio held at the 1958 Round Table Conference of the International Economic Association. The conference participants, arguing on the basis of the same empirical evidence, could not reach agreement. However,

> it was generally acknowledged, of course, that year-to-year changes in the ratio are strongly influenced by the position of the year in the trade cycle, years of depression showing a relatively high, and years of boom a relatively low capital-output ratio. For the purpose of determining whether the ratio tends to stability or not, averages over longer periods must be taken.

In this respect the agreement ended:

> The ratio of the Net Capital Stock to the Net National Product calculated by Kuznets for the United States (see Professor Domar's paper[19]) moved from 3.2 on the average over the twenty years 1869–1888 to 3.4 over the next twenty years and 3.6 over the following twenty. After that (in the period 1939–1955) it came down to 2.9.

Some participants were inclined to minimize the significance of such small changes over such long periods. Others argued that "by its very nature the average capital coefficient is a sluggish animal" because even large changes in the incremental ratio will produce only small changes in the average ratio, so that changes of 24 percent (from maximum to minimum) in the latter must be considered large. Luts himself sided with the second group, with the additional reason that he has not so far been able to find a convincing theoretical explanation of why the capital/output ratio should remain stable.

Supposing that K/Y and P/Y are constants, the constancy in the rate of profits on capital is explained—namely,

$$\frac{P}{K} = \left(\frac{P}{Y}\right) \Big/ \left(\frac{K}{Y}\right) = \text{constant}.$$

As was argued above, historical constancies in the rate of profit on capital and in the capital/output ratio do not seem to be demonstrable. If we break down the assumption of either the constancy of P/Y or of K/Y, we cannot keep the $(P/Y)/(K/Y)$ constant, without successful offsetting one by the other.

Three to four decades have passed since the discussion of historical constancies. The focus in this book is changes of some variables in relation to the business cycle. The observation periods in Chapter 2 were twenty-two years (in most cases), and the timespan covered by the discussion here is not 100 years but at most four decades or so after World War II.

During these periods we cannot recognize the stability of the relative shares, the capital/output ratio, and the profit rate on capital:

- The relative share of labor was increasing during the period 1953 to 1975 and then decreasing for about ten years in the United Kingdom (see Figure 2.2a in Chapter 2, and Iyoda, 1985, fig. 1). Japanese labor share has also increasing and decreasing periods, though the periods are shorter than those in the United Kingdom: For example, decreasing from 1953 to 1961 and increasing from 1970 to 1975 (see Figure 2.4a in Chapter 2, and Iyoda, 1987, fig. 1).
- The capital/output ratio[20] had an increasing trend from 0.7 (1960) to 1.8 (1992) in Japan (Economic Planning Agency, 1993, fig. 2-2-4).
- The profit rate changes greatly during the business cycle (see Figures 2.5a 2.5b, 2.6, and 2.7 in Chapter 2).

CONCLUSIONS: SOME REMARKS ON KALDOR'S MODEL

This chapter has explained Kaldor's model of income distribution and has reformulated his model by using additional identities, interpreting it in both the short run and the long run. The discussion referred to various comments on it for theoretical development and also historical constancies that Kaldor recognized. The following conclusions can be made:

1. According to the Keynesian hypothesis, Kaldor treats the investment/output ratio as an independent variable, which plays a strategic role in determining the distributive shares of income. The model shows the share of profits P/Y, the rate of profits on capital P/vY, and the real wage rate W/L as functions of I/Y, which in turn determined independently of P/Y or W/L. Kaldor considers that savings and investment equilibrium will be accomplished through the change of distributive shares—namely, equivalent savings to investment (which is given independently) are generated through the change of distributive shares.

Considering the following aspects of capitalist societies, this Kaldor's treatment is plausible: (1) wage contracts are made not in terms of real wage rate but money wage rate, (2) economic actors of investment and savings are not always the same: entrepreneurs who act as investors cannot decide directly the profit rate but can decide themselves the volume of investment, (3) therefore investment decisions of entrepreneurs make a strategic factor in determining the share of profits, the rate of profit, and the real wage rate in the capitalist society. In this respect, I support this Kaldor's treatment.

2. Suppose that the investment/output ratio increases under full employment in the short run. Then it turns out that the relative share of profits ρ_c will increase, and the profit rate on capital π will also increase. However, the real wage rate will decrease. Assuming nonnegative growth of the money wage rate, it turns out that the economy faces a possibile increase in the share of profits leading to an increase in the money wage rate, which in turn results in a high rate of price increase.

A logical relationship has been explained for changes of ρ_c, π, ω, and e under full employment in the long run, and Kaldor's model has been dealt with without considering equilibrium values. However, to explain fully changes of ρ_c, π, ω, and e, a growth theory is needed that incorporates technological changes into the theory.

3. Kaldor recognized the "historical constancy" of the distributive shares and felt that the model should be constructed to account for these. He (1957b) presented three kinds of historical constancies—the relative shares, the capital/output ratio, and the rate of profit on capital.

However, according to the above discussions about these constancies, the results were rather negative to them. The focus here is on changes of economic variables in relation to the business cycle, and the observation periods are not 100 years or more but a few decades—at most, four decades. We cannot find these constancies during our observation periods. In these respects, our standpoint differs from Kaldor's intention on the background for model construction.

4. Among various comments on Kaldor's model, one of the weakest points of his model is that it cannot explain the distribution of income in an underemployment economy. His equation (2), which explains the distributive shares under full employment, has two unknown variables in an underemployment economy. In reply to this weakness, some Keynesians introduced the *first postulate of the classical theory* and completed the model. I present alternative models from different viewpoints in the next chapter.

APPENDIX 3A: A NEOCLASSICAL MODEL OF INCOME DISTRIBUTION—IN COMPARISON WITH KALDOR'S MODEL

This appendix compares Kaldor's model and a neoclassical model of income distribution, which is almost a reproduction of Iyoda (1975).

A Model

First, this standard neoclassical model of income distribution follows Samuelson and Modigliani (1996a, pp. 271–272). The equations here are numbered to correspond to Kaldor's in the "Interpretation" section of this chapter for comparative convenience.

Let total real output be produced by labor L and by total homogeneous capital K. For simplicity, the production of consumption output O_c and of net capital formation $\dot{K} = dK/dt$ is assumed to involve the same capital-labor factor intensities. This results in the following constant-returns-to-scale function:

$$Y = O_c + \dot{K} = F(K, L). \tag{N-1}$$

Equation (N-1), in view of its first-degree homogeneity property, can be rewritten as

$$y = F(k, 1) = f(k), \ \partial F(k, 1)/\partial k = f'(k) > 0 \tag{N-1'}$$

where

$$y = Y/L,$$
$$k = K/L,$$

with $d^2f(k)/dk^2 = f''(k) < 0$ in consequence of diminishing returns.

We assume neoclassical smoothness and substitutability and perfect markets, under which conditions competition will enforce at all times equality of factor prices to factor marginal productivities.

The profit rate π is

$$\pi = \frac{P}{K} = \frac{\partial F(K, L)}{\partial K} = f'(k), \text{ and} \tag{N-b}$$

the real wage rate ω is

$$\omega = \frac{W}{L} = \frac{Y - \pi K}{L}$$
$$= f(k) - kf'(k). \tag{N-c}$$

The relative share of property and the price level respectively expressed as

$$\rho_c = \frac{P}{Y} = \frac{k(\partial Y/\partial K)}{\partial Y/\partial L + k(\partial Y/\partial K)} \text{ and} \tag{N-2-1}$$

$$e = \frac{\omega_m}{\omega}. \tag{N-d}$$

When L and K are given under neoclassical assumptions, marginal productivity of capital and labor are given respectively according to the production function. This results in the real wage rate, the relative share of property (capital), and the profit rate. For given ω_m, we also have the price level from equation (N-d).

Features of the Model

The model has the following features:

- The real wage rate and the relative share of labor are determined by the technical condition (expressed by the production function) and the capital intensity k.
- Two savings propensities, s_p and s_w, have no direct relationship in determining the real wage rate ω, the relative share of property ρ_c, the profit rate π, and the price level e.
- Capital K is expressed in physical terms. However, when capital is expressed in value terms, the profit rate π will vary with the method of measurement (based on replacement cost or a book value).

Savings S are expressed as

$$\begin{aligned} S &= s_w W + s_p P \\ &= s_w \omega L + s_p \pi K. \end{aligned}$$

In the neoclassical model, ω and π are given by the respective marginal product $(\partial F/\partial L,\ \partial F/\partial K)$ according to the production function. Investment I becomes equal to this S through the change of interest rate in the capital market $(I \rightarrow S)$.

However, Kaldor does not take profit maximization principles. ω and π are respectively given by $\mu(1 - \rho_c)$ and ρ_c/v, both of which depend on ρ_c (see "Interpretations" in this chapter). Investment I is given independently in Kaldor's model, then S becomes equal to this given I through the changes of the distributive shares $(S \rightarrow I)$.

Capital is assumed homogeneous in the neoclassical model. So there is no problem between the models in physical terms and in value terms. When capital is not homogeneous, a couple of questions appear in measuring capital. However, Kaldor is free from these questions. The profit rate is compatible with various methods of measuring capital, and it is easy to construct a model in nominal terms.

NOTES

1. This is in line with the idea of *widow's cruse* in determining the profits. Profits are likened to a widow's cruse in Keynes's *Treatise on Money* (1930, p. 125):

If entrepreneurs choose to spend a portion of their profits on consumption (and there is, of course, nothing to prevent them from doing this), the effect is to *increase* the profits on the sale of liquid consumption goods by an amount exactly equal to the amount of profits which have been thus expended. . . . Thus profits, as a source of capital increment for entrepreneurs, are a widow's cruse which remains undepleted however much of them may be devoted to riotous living.

Referring to this passage, Kaldor (1955–1956, p. 227 n. 1) puts an emphasis on that "here Keynes regards entrepreneurial incomes as being the resultant of their expenditure decisions, rather than the other way round—which is perhaps the most important difference between 'Keynesian' and 'pre-Keynesian' habits of thought."

In connection with the multiplier, Kaldor (1955–1956, p. 228 n. 2) also refers to Robinson (1956) and Kalecki (1942). Kaldor mentions that he owed "a great deal of stimulus to a paper by Kalecki, 'A Theory of Profits,' whose approach is in some ways reminiscent of the widow's cruse of Keynes' Treatise."

Kalecki (1945) explains widow's cruse idea clearly in Chapter 3, The Determinants of Profits, which was developed back in 1935 in his "Essai d'une théorie de mouvement cyclique des affairs," *Revue d'Economie Politique* (March–April 1935), and his "A Macrodynamic Theory of Business Cycles," *Econometrica* (July 1935). Kalecki (1945, p. 46) says that "It is clear that capitalists may decide to consume and to invest more in a given period than in the preceding one, but they cannot decide to earn more. It is, therefore, their investment and consumption decisions which determine profits, and not vice versa."

2. Refer to Harrod (1948, lecture 3). According to Harrod, the warranted rate of growth G_w is the growth rate of output that warrants a savings-investment equilibrium under optimum utilization of capital. This is expressed as

$$G_w = s/c_r,$$

where c_r = the required capital coefficient $I/\Delta Y$.

3. Kaldor (1955–1956, p. 232) says that "this does not mean that there will be an inherent tendency to a smooth rate of growth in a capitalist economy." Problems of the trade cycle lie outside the purposes of this book. However, he explains it as follows:

The causes of cyclical movements should be sought in a disharmony between the entrepreneurs' *desired* growth rate (as influenced by the degree of optimism and the volatility of expectations) that governs the rate of increase of output capacity G, and the natural growth rate G' (dependent on technical progress and growth of the working population) that governs the rate of growth in output over longer periods. Then it is the excess of G over G'—not the excess of s over $G'v$—that causes periodic breakdowns in the investment process. Refer to Kaldor (1957a, pp. 251–254) for a further discussion.

4. Refer to Iyoda (1975) for a similar discussion. See Appendix 3A for a comparison with a neoclassical model of income distribution.

5. The relative share of profits ρ_c is nonnegative, and Kaldor sets a condition,

$$1 \geq s_p > s_w \geq 0$$

for fully operating the model. Then $C > s_w$. In case of $C < s_w$, ρ_c then the profit rate π becomes negative.

Kaldor (1955–1956, p. 229 n. 1) says on $s_p > s_w$ that "This may be assumed . . . simply as a consequence of the fact that the bulk of profits accrues in the form of company profits and a high proportion of companies' marginal profits is put to reserve." So there is support for a view that this is a plausible condition.

An inequality $C > s_w$ became one of the focal points between Pasinetti (1962) and Samuelson and Modigliani (1966a).

Kaldor (1966a, p. 312) later says, "From the point of view of the mechanics of a Keynesian model, it is *gross* savings out of *gross* profits, and *gross* investment, that are relevant, not *net* savings and *net* investment." He himself makes a remark on inequality $C > s_w$, which was "the original postulate of my 'Keynesian' distribution theory" (1978, p. xv). This is a plausible assumption, in particular under *full employment*, though the condition was not stated explicitly in his original model.

We also consider that this condition will still holds true of the underemployment economy. We shall construct our Kaldorian models in gross terms in the next chapter. Condition $C > s_w$ will become more plausible in this treatment. For the same volume of depreciation is included in both numerator and denominator.

6. This W is different from Kaldor's original model, where $W = \omega L$. Kaldor treats W/L as the real wage rate in the model (1955–1956, p. 232). Two remarks can be made in relation to this. First, considering this Kaldor's treatment, his notations are in real terms (at constant price). As far as arguments are made in the ratio, it does not seem to make any difference between nominal and real terms. I will develop his discussion in nominal terms. This treatment is important because I do not examine the classical dichotomy (for a further argument, refer to "The Classical Dichotomy" in Chapter 5).

Second, the real wage identity above is a much-simplified version of reality. One aggregate product (possibly based on the national income) is considered in the model. The price level e here is not exactly the same as consumer (or retail) prices. For a more accurate discussion, it may be possible to take the national income deflator as price level e and the consumer (or retail) price index as the consumer prices, respectively. The same arguments hold true of the real wage identity used in Chapter 4.

7. Price level e here will have no effect on the ratio of I/Y, for

$$\frac{I}{Y} = \frac{eI_r}{e\mu L} = \frac{I_r}{\mu L},$$

where I_r = investment in real terms.
Therefore, according to equation (2), given s_p and s_w, ρ_c is independent from price level e.

The next is the capital/output ratio. If $K_v = eK$, by above equation (a) v is also independent from e; however, if K_v = the historical cost, v will be affected by e.

Then, by above equation (b) we can discuss the effect of price level on the profit rate, which depends on the method of measuring capital.

8. Changes of the investment/output growth ratio are decomposed into per capita investment growth and per capita productivity growth as follows:

$$C = \frac{I}{Y} = \frac{eI_r}{e\mu L},$$

where I_r = investment in real terms. Then

$$C = \frac{i_r}{\mu}, \tag{e}$$

where $i_r = I_r/L$.

From this, we have a growth rate form

$$\hat{C} = \hat{\imath}_r - \hat{\mu}. \tag{e'}$$

9. See the discussion in "Historical Constancies" in this chapter for details.

10. See "Historical Constancies" in the chapter for a simple explanation of his technical production function.

11. Refer to polemic papers in the *Review of Economic Studies* 96 (October 1966). For example, Samuelson and Modigliani (1966a, 1966b), and Solow (1966) were on the MIT and Harvard side; Pasinetti (1966), Robinson (1966), and Kaldor (1966a) were on the U.K. Cambridge side. Refer to note 27 of Chapter 2 for some arguments in relation to Solow (1966).

Kaldor (1966a, p. 315) clearly expresses two reasons that he rejects the marginal productivity approach:

(i) All empirical studies concerning the short period relationship between output and employment (at least in manufacturing activities) show the elasticity of the former with regard to changes in the latter to be greater, not less, than unity ("Okun's Law" makes it 3 [Okun (1962)], which implies of course that the short-period marginal product of labour exceeds the average product. . . . (ii) All empirical studies concerning the relationship of productivity and production (again, for manufacturing activities) reveal the existence of (long-run) increasing returns, both on account of the economies of large-scale production, and of the subdivision of processes (and industries) with an increase in the scale of activities.

More or less same arguments are seen in Kaldor (1960a, 1960b), which are a rejoinder to Atsumi (1960) and Tobin (1960) and to Findlay (1960), respectively. Furthermore, refer to Kaldor (1961, pp. 203–208) for his views of rejecting the production function. Robinson (1953–1954, 1967) also basically shares with Kaldor these views of marginal productivity and production function, though there are some differences between them.

12. See Kaldor (1957a, p. 251 n. 1) for the discussion in relation to these. Kaldor (1961) constructs a model denoting s_p and s_w as the propensity to save out of profits and wages, respectively.

13. See Weintraub (1958, p. 105). A similar argument is seen in Watanabe (1960).

14. For some of these examples, refer to note 2 in Chapter 1.

15. For the distributive shares, Kaldor quotes Brown and Hart (1952) for the United Kingdom and Kuznets (1952) for the United States.

For the capital/output ratio, he quotes Brown and Weber (1953) for the United Kingdom, Maywald (1956) for Great Britain, and Fellner (1947, table 3) based on Kuznets estimates for the United States.

For the rate of profit on capital, he quotes Brown and Weber (1953) for the United Kingdom and Kuznets (1952) for the United States.

16. Refer to Iyoda (1971b) for arguments on the model.

17. Kaldor (1961, p. 179) says that none of these facts can be plausibly explained by the theoretical construction of neoclassical theory. The purpose of his paper (1961) was to present a model of income distribution and capital accumulation that is capable of explaining at least some of these stylized facts.

18. These figures in percentage are stable (around 55) during the years 1870 to 1884, then become higher (around 60) during the years 1890 to 1904, and far higher (around 64 to 69) during the years 1924 to 1933 and 1948 to 1950. But during the World War II period they are around 60.

19. For example, see Domar (1961, table 5). Kravis (1959) shows that the capital/output ratio has been increasing from around the year 1900 to the 1930s, and then decreasing to the 1950s in the United States.

20. The capital/output ratio is calculated by gross capital stock to gross national product (at constant prices).

4. KALDORIAN MODELS: TWO APPLIED MODELS

This chapter deals with a model of income distribution and explains some of the facts established in Chapter 2. Two models are applied to an underemployment economy based on Kaldor's idea. The chapter's premise is that underemployment is a more general economic situation than full employment. However, Kaldor's original model is not able to explain income distribution in an underemployment economy. The prime aim of his original model was to explain the relative stability of the distributive shares in a full-employment economy. Hence, the model lacks an equation that determines the volume of employment or the volume of output in an underemployment economy. Establishing a model of income distribution in that economy is needed to explain the change of the distributive shares and some other relational variables in the various phases of the business cycle.

There might be a couple of ways to complete his model as a general model that includes an underemployment economy. One of the ways taken by some Keynesians[1] is to introduce "the first postulate of the classical theory of employment" (Keynes, 1936, p. 5), which means the wage rate is determined by the marginal productivity of labor. They express the function (based on profit-maximization principles) as

$$Y = F(L), \quad \text{where} \quad \omega = \partial Y / \partial L.$$

However, Kaldor does not concur with this direction. He does not use profit-maximization principles for building his model. There are alternative ways to complete it as a macro model in his line, without introducing the first postulate of the classical. One way is to introduce an equation in which the volume of labor force employed is determined by the volume of investment, and the other is to introduce a kind of markup pricing equation. We might call the former an *employment decision* approach and the other a *markup pricing approach*.

I completed a model by using the latter approach in 1976 and discuss it in the section called "Model B: A Markup Pricing Approach" in this chapter. The model is applied to an underemployment economy and explains some established facts from the previous chapter.

In the section called "Model A: An Employment Decision Approach," a model based on the employment decision approach is presented and discussed. Then in the section on "Model B" a model based on the markup pricing approach is presented and discussed. Finally, tentative conclusions about the two models are drawn with some remarks on both approaches.

MODEL A: AN EMPLOYMENT DECISION APPROACH

This section begins with the background needed to construct a macroeconomic model of income distribution that includes an underemployment economy. First, an equation that relates the volume of employment to that of investment is introduced as an *employment decision* approach. Second, an equation is introduced that shows that an increase in employment results in growth in labor productivity in an underemployment economy and a decrease in investment results in a reverse case. The equation takes into consideration that productivity shows a sharp increase in the first year of expansion and a relative decrease (or a negative growth) in the first year of contraction. These equations are explained in more detail later.

These two assumptions are used to present a very simple model that explains the change of the distribution-related variables in the business cycle.

The model and its subsequent solution are presented together with an analysis of comparative statics to investigate the changes of the relative share, the real wage rate, and the profit rate.

Assumptions and Notations

Assumptions

Model A requires the following assumptions:

i. A closed private economy is assumed.
ii. One product (or an aggregate product based on national income) is assumed.
iii. The amount of capital stock and the number of workers are given in the short run.
iv. Increase in investment increases the number of workers employed in an underemployment economy, and decrease in investment decreases the number of workers employed.

v. Increase in investment causes the growth of labor productivity in an under-employment economy, and a decrease of investment causes a decline in labor productivity.[2]

Notations[3]

This section uses virtually the same notations as Kaldor but refers to variables in both nominal and gross terms. For nominal terms, we do not use the classical dichotomy, aiming at dealing with the effect of the money wage rate on other macroeconomic variables. For gross terms, an estimation of depreciation, under the economy of high technical progress and rapid inflation, is difficult, which means that an accurate division of gross profits between depreciation and net profits is difficult to ascertain. Also for gross terms, at the corporate level, the replacement is usually combined with new investment and the prices of capital goods are subject to changes.

Y = output	W = wages
P = profits	I = investment
S = savings	D = depreciation
L = labor force employed	K_v = value of capital
ω_m = money wage rate	ω = real wage rate
e = price level	μ = labor productivity per head

s_p *and* s_w = propensity to save from profits and wages (and salaries), respectively

Subscripts $_{fk}$ and $_{fl}$ = full employment of capital and full employment of the labor force, respectively (for example, L_{fk} denotes the number of labor force employed under full employment of capital; L_{fl} the number of labor fully-employed).

Model A

We build a model (A) as follows:

Distribution of Output	$Y \equiv W + P$	(1)
Savings-Investment Equilibrium	$I \equiv S$	(2)
Total Savings	$S \equiv s_w W + s_p P$	(3)
Employment-Investment Function	$L = a + b\,(I - I^*)$	(4)
Productivity-Employment Function	$\mu = c + h\,(L - L^*)$	(5)
Total Output	$Y \equiv e\mu L$	(6)
Wages Paid	$W \equiv \omega_m L$	(7)

Equations (1)–(3) are identities which are the same as those in Kaldor (we also assume simple savings functions $S_w = s_w W$ and $S_p = s_p P$). Equations (6)–(7) are identities.

Equations (4) and (5) need further explanation. In equation (4), the number of labor force is showed as a function of investment. I^* means the amount of investment which sustains the present number of labor employed. This would be greater than depreciation due to technical progress. Apart from technical progress, I^* equals the amount of D under a simple reproduction which we call a stationary state. L^* denotes the number of labor force employed in the case of $I = I^*$.

If an actual investment is larger than I^*, the volume of employment grows. If, on the contrary, the actual investment is smaller than I^*, the volume of employment decreases. This relationship is stated in the following way:

$$L^* = a \qquad \text{if} \quad I = I^*,$$

$$L = a + b(I - I^*) \quad \text{if} \quad I \le I_{fl},$$

where

$$L' < 0 \quad \text{for} \quad I < I^*, \quad \text{and}$$

$$L' > 0 \quad \text{for} \quad I^* < I < I_{fl}.$$

Equation (5) is based on assumption v. In an underemployment economy, the increase of employment causes the growth of labor productivity until the full employment of capital,[4] and the decrease of employment causes negative or slow growth in productivity. However, it is not necessary to consider literally full employment of capital in physical terms. We consider it as a normal operation rate of capital (or as the turning point below which the result would be a decrease of labor productivity). Considering technical progress, an absolute decrease in μ would be alleviated, and then its growth would slow or decrease.

Then we have

$$\mu = c + h(L - L^*) \qquad \text{if} \quad L \le L_{fk}$$

where

$\mu' > 0 \quad$ for $\quad L^* < L,$
$\mu' \le 0$ (without technical progress) $\quad$ for $\quad L \le L^*$, and
$\mu' \ge 0 \quad$ or $\quad \mu' < 0$ (with technical progress) $\quad$ for $\quad L < L^*.$

A model consisting of equations (1) to (7) will now be examined.

Suppose that I, as an independent variable following Kaldor's treatment (that is, the Keynesian hypothesis), and the other nine variables shown below are given. The number of unknown variables is equal to 7. The seven equations allow the model to have a solution. The relationship is articulated as follows:

1 independent variable	I
9 given variables	s_w, s_p, a, b, I^*, c, h, L^*, and ω_m
7 unknown variables	Y, W, P, S, L, μ, and e
7 equations (including identities)	(1) to (7)

This model is similar to Kaldor's. Using equations (1) to (3) results in Kaldor's equation, which explains the relative share of property ρ_c:

$$\rho_c = \frac{I}{Y(s_p - s_w)} - \frac{s_w}{s_p - s_w}.$$

However, this model is different in the following two points: (1) variables are expressed in both nominal and gross terms, and (2) supposing an under-employment economy, two functions (4) and (5) are added to complete the model.

Model A: A Solution and Restraint Conditions

A Solution[5]

By using equations (1) to (4) and (7), we have

$$Y = \frac{I + (s_p - s_w)\omega_m X}{s_p}, \tag{a}$$

$$W = \omega_m X, \text{ and} \tag{b}$$

$$P = \frac{I - s_w \omega_m X}{s_p}, \tag{c}$$

where

$$X = a + b(I - I^*).$$

The number of labor force employed L is independently determined by equation (4) and then substituting this L by X.

Then e is obtained by using (a) and equations (4) to (6):

$$e = \frac{I + (s_p - s_w)\omega_m X}{s_p\{c + h(X - L^*)\}X} \tag{d}$$

ρ_c, ω, and π, in which we have an analytical interest, are expressed in an identity form, respectively:

$$\rho_c \equiv P/Y, \tag{8}$$

$$\omega \equiv \omega_m/e, \text{ and} \tag{9}$$

$$\pi \equiv P/K_v. \tag{10}$$

Substituting (a), (c), and (d) for Y, P, and e in equations (8) to (10), respectively, we have

$$\rho_c = \frac{I - s_w \omega_m X}{I + (s_p - s_w)\omega_m X}, \tag{8-1}$$

$$\omega = \frac{s_p \omega_m \{c + h(X - L^*)\} X}{I + (s_p - s_w)\omega_m X}, \text{ and} \tag{9-1}$$

$$\pi = \frac{I - s_w \omega_m X}{s_p K_v}. \tag{10-1}$$

By observation, we know both I and ω_m are all related to ρ_c, ω, and π, respectively. However, labor productivity μ has no direct relationship to the property share ρ_c and the profit rate π but relates to price level e and also to the real wage rate ω. (Consider { } of numerator in (9-1) to be the same as equation (5), which means μ).

Restraint Conditions to the Model

In addition to Kaldor's condition

$$1 \geq s_p > s_w \geq 0$$

for fully operating the model, the model must satisfy the following two conditions:

- The real wage rate is above a certain subsistence minimum level,[6] and
- All variables are nonnegative.

Since $P > 0$ in (c),

$$I - s_w \omega_m X > 0. \tag{i}$$

The first condition is the one by which variables in the model are assured to have a plausible (economic) meaning. Investment is dealt with in the gross term, so we do not take up negative investment.

Model A: An Analysis in Comparative Statics[7]

Dealing with investment I and the money wage rate ω_m as strategic factors (investment could be a policy variable), we make an analysis in comparative statics aiming at seeing the effect of the change of I and ω_m on ρ_c, ω, and π, respectively.

Take I and ω_m as strategic variables and other variables as exogenous ones (given or constant):

2 strategic variables I and ω_m
9 exogenous variables (given and constant) s_w, s_p, a, b, I^*, c, h, L^*, and K_v

The Profit (Property) Share

A growth rate formula of the property share can be obtained from (8-1):

$$\hat{\rho}_c = \frac{s_p\omega_m I\{\hat{I}(X - bI) - \hat{\omega}_m X\}}{\{I + (s_p - s_w)\omega_m X\}(I - s_w\omega_m X)}, \tag{8-1'}$$

where $\dot{\rho}_c$ and $\hat{\rho}_c$ represent $d\rho_c/dt$ and $\dot{\rho}_c/\rho_c$, respectively.

Since the denominator is positive under our constraint conditions above, we have:

CASE I. ($\hat{I}$, $\hat{\omega}_m > 0$). Suppose that $X - bI > 0$ of equation (8-1').[8] Making some arrangements on this numerator, we have

$$\frac{\hat{I}}{\hat{\omega}_m} \gtreqless \frac{X}{X - bI} \quad \Rightarrow \quad \text{Numerator} \gtreqless 0.$$

Then

$$\frac{\hat{I}}{\hat{\omega}_m} \gtreqless \frac{X}{X - bI} \quad \Rightarrow \quad \hat{\rho}_c \gtreqless 0.$$

CASE II. ($\hat{I} < 0$, $\hat{\omega}_m > 0$). Always $\hat{\rho}_c < 0$.

The Real Wage Rate

The growth rate formula of the real wage rate is obtained from (9-1):

$$\hat{\omega} = \frac{I}{\{c + h(X - L^*)\}\{I + (s_p - s_w)\omega_m X\}}\left[-\frac{\hat{I}}{X}((a - bI^*) \times (c - hL^*) + hX[a - b\{I + I^* + (s_p - s_w)\omega_m X\}]) + \hat{\omega}_m\{c + h(X - L^*)\}\right]. \tag{9-1'}$$

Since all variables are positive, the denominator of the equation (9-1') is positive (see solution e of (d), for example).

Concerning the numerator of equation (9-1'):

CASE I. ($\hat{I}$, $\hat{\omega}_m > 0$). Let

$$V = (a - bI^*)(c - hL^*) + hX[a - b\{I + I^* + (s_p - s_w)\omega_m X\}].^{9}$$

Then we have, for $V > 0$

$$\frac{\hat{\omega}_m}{\hat{I}} \gtreqless \frac{V}{X\{c + h(X - L^*)\}} \quad \Rightarrow \quad \text{Numerator} \gtreqless 0.$$

Therefore, for $V > 0$

$$\frac{\hat{\omega}_m}{\hat{I}} \gtreqless \frac{V}{X\{c + h(X - L^*)\}} \quad \Rightarrow \quad \hat{\omega} \gtreqless 0.$$

CASE II. $(\hat{I} < 0,\ \hat{\omega}_m > 0)$.

$\hat{\omega} > 0$, if $V > 0$.

CASE III. $(\hat{I} > 0,\ \hat{\omega}_m > 0)$.

$\hat{\omega} > 0$, if $V < 0$.

CASE IV. $(\hat{I} < 0,\ \hat{\omega}_m > 0)$. If $V < 0$, then

$$\frac{\hat{\omega}_m}{\hat{I}} \lesseqgtr \frac{V}{X\{c + h(X - L^*)\}} \quad \Rightarrow \quad \hat{\omega} \gtreqless 0.$$

The Profit Rate

The growth rate formula of the profit rate is obtained from (10-1).

$$\hat{\pi} = \frac{I\hat{I}(1 - bs_w\omega_m) - \hat{\omega}_m s_w \omega_m X}{I - s_w\omega_m X}. \tag{10-1'}$$

Since $(1 - bs_w\omega_m)$ is considered as positive,[10] we have

CASE I. $(\hat{I},\ \hat{\omega}_m > 0)$.

$$\frac{\hat{I}}{\hat{\omega}_m} \gtreqless \frac{s_w\omega_m X}{I(1 - bs_w\omega_m)} \quad \Rightarrow \quad \hat{\pi} \gtreqless 0.$$

CASE II. $(\hat{I} < 0,\ \hat{\omega}_m > 0)$. Always $\hat{\pi} < 0$.

To see a general prospect of the change of this profit rate, we put back

$$\frac{s_w\omega_m X}{I(1 - bs_w\omega_m)}$$ [11]

into the original form. We have

$$\frac{s_w W}{s_p P + s_w\omega_m(L - bI)}.$$

As we discussed in the previous note, b is tiny, and the figure bI is not large enough against the figure L. So $L - bI$ is close to L, which means $\omega_m(L - bI)$ is close to $\omega_m L$ $(= W)$. Then the denominator is nearly equal to investment I. Hence we consider π would increase at a fairly low ratio of $\hat{I}$ to $\hat{\omega}_m$.

By comparative statics, we examined the effect of investment and the money wage rate on the relative share, the real wage rate, and the profit rate, respectively. Results of the analysis in comparative statics under our assumptions are first, ρ_c would increase, if the ratio of $\hat{I}$ to $\hat{\omega}_m$ is greater than $X/(X - bI)$. ρ_c would decrease in the reverse case (where $\hat{I} > 0$), or if the growth rate of I is negative ($\hat{I} < 0$) under depression or a sluggish situation.

Second, the growth rate of ω is determined in accordance with the growth rate ratio of ω_m to I. Various cases on terms are possible.

Finally, the growth rate of π is determined by the growth rate ratio of I to ω_m; however, π would increase at a fairly low growth rate ratio. For the figure of $s_w\omega_m X/I(1 - bs_w\omega_m)$ is fairly small.

A Brief Summary: Concluding Remarks on Model A

The following summary discusses the model's explanation of the established facts contained in Chapter 2.

1. A simple equation in which L was shown as a function of I was introduced in order to apply Kaldor's model of income distribution to an underemployment economy in the short run. This model is in line with Kaldor's approach, which excludes the profit-maximization principle (the marginal productivity theory). The assumption was that an increase of I, which causes an increase of L, would increase labor productivity in an underemployment economy; a decrease of I, which causes a decrease of L, would decrease labor productivity.

2. By using this simple Model A, an analysis in comparative statics aimed at stating a few policy relevances. Considering I as a policy variable, ω_m as an exogenous variable, and all others as constant, the effects of I and ω_m on ρ_c, ω, and π, respectively, were examined.

3. The analysis showed that an increase of I would generally bring a respective increase of ρ_c and π, although the more accurate description was stated in each case by the respective formula.

a. If $\hat{I} > 0$ and $\hat{\omega}_m > 0$ (case i), ρ_c will increase at a fairly low growth rate ratio of I to ω_m exceeding $X/(X - bI)$, which explains a phase of expansion in the business cycle. Case ii—$\hat{I} < 0$ and $\hat{\omega}_m > 0$, in which ρ_c decreases—explains a phase of contraction.

b. Various cases for the growth rate of ω are possibilities, depending on the cases stated. There were no common features of the change of ω between the three countries.

c. If $\hat{I} > 0$ and $\hat{\omega}_m > 0$ (case i), π grows at a fairly low growth rate ratio of I to ω_m, for the figure of

$$s_w\omega_m X/I(1 - bs_w\omega_m)$$

is fairly small. This explains a phase of expansion in the business cycle. Case ii—$\hat{I} < 0$ and $\hat{\omega}_m > 0$, in which π decreases—explains a phase of contraction in the business cycle.

The model has the possibility of explaining the countercyclical change of the labor share to the business cycle and the procyclical change of the profit rate to it as well.

4. Another function of this model is explaining a rapid growth in labor productivity in the first expansion year after the slump, due to the increase of the operation rate of capital caused by the growth of I in an underemployment economy. On the contrary, it would also explain the relative slowdown in μ in the first contraction year after the boom. It seems possible to explain these symmetrical facts in relation to the change of μ. But this characteristic is simply caused by assumption v of the model, in which the change in productivity was related to that of investment.

5. On the other hand, it is clear that the model is too simple in explaining the facts of the real economy. Some refinements would be necessary, for example, for functions (4) and (5). Presenting a complicated macro model might be possible. However, it becomes difficult to illustrate fundamental relationships in such a simple way.

MODEL B: A MARKUP PRICING APPROACH

Introduction

The other alternative approach to extending Kaldor's model of income distribution to an underemployment economy is to introduce a price-setting equation as follows:

$$Y = (1 + r)(W + D). \tag{4a}$$

This equation means that entrepreneurs set a price by marking up on wages plus depreciation at a customary rate of r, supposing that this price is generally realized on a macro level. It is an alternative assumption based on Kaldor's approach in which he does not assume perfect competition and profit-maximization principles.

Iyoda (1976) completed a model by introducing equation (4a) and made an analysis in comparative statics.[12] The result was that when investment increased, relative share of property would decrease but profit rate would increase. The real wage rate would change in the relationship between the growth rates of investment and the money wage rate. The policy implication was fairly interesting. These possibilities might exist in an economy; however, many of the estimates of the relative income shares have shown that the share of property would increase when investment grew. My estimates were similar with those for Japan.

The reason that the increase of investment brings the decrease of the relative share of property is found in equation (4a). Equation (4a) is based on a kind of full-cost principle, in which profits are gained at a *customary rate* to the cost. In the previous model, depreciation D was dealt with as constant. The increase of the money wage rate reflected on price and then the volume of output. But D itself did not affect the change of price, which meant the profit margins from D were constant as $D \cdot r$. That is to say, the capital cost decreased relatively as an increase of investment brought the increase of output.

Suppose that D is adjusted for the price change. Then

$$D = e\delta K, \tag{11}$$

where δ = rate of depreciation of capital.

With respect to the labor productivity, it first is taken as an exogenous variable. This treatment is for the sake of simplification in an analytical explanation. As is shown later, the model can be completed by using a productivity-employment function.

Assumptions and Notations

Assumptions i, ii, and iii are borrowed from Model A, and iv(a) is substituted for Model A's iv.

i. A closed private economy is assumed.
ii. One output (or an aggregate product based on national income) is assumed.
iii. The amount of capital stock and the number of workers are given in the short run.
iv(a). A price is set by marking up on wages and depreciation at a customary rate of r, supposing that this price is generally realized on a macro level.

We keep on the same notations as those used in Model A.

Model B

We have equation (4a) instead of the previous equation (4) and remove equation (5) in Model A. Adding identity (11), we have a following model (B):[13]

$$Y \equiv W + P \tag{1}$$

$$I \equiv S \tag{2}$$

$$S \equiv s_w W + s_p P \tag{3}$$

$$Y = (1 + r)(W + D) \tag{4a}$$

$$Y \equiv e\mu L \tag{6}$$

$$W \equiv \omega_m L \tag{7}$$

$$D \equiv e\delta K \tag{11}$$

If these are treated as in Model A, this is a complete system and provides a solution. Suppose that I, as the independent variable, and other seven variables as stated below are given. Then the number of unknown variables is seven. Because we have seven equations, the model has a solution.

The relationship is expressed as follows:

1 independent variable	I
7 exogenous variables	s_w, s_p, r, μ, ω_m, δ, and K
7 unknown variables	Y, W, P, S, D, L, and e
7 equations (including identities)	(1)–(4a), (6)–(7), and (11)

This model is similar to that of Kaldor's in Model A. By using equations (1) to (3), Kaldor's equation is available to explain the relative income share of property. The model is addressed in both nominal and gross terms as in Model A. Unlike in Model A, however a markup pricing equation is used instead of employment-investment, assuming the underemployment economy.

Model B: A Solution and Restraint Conditions

A Solution

It is difficult to have as a simple solution for Model B as that for Model A. L and e are obtained by using equations (1) to (4a), (6) to (7), and (11):[14]

$$L = \frac{A - B \pm \sqrt{Z}}{2(s_p r + s_w)\omega_m \mu}, \tag{e}$$

$$e = \frac{A + B \pm \sqrt{Z}}{2(1 + r)\delta K \cdot s_p \mu}, \tag{d-1}$$

where

$$A = I\mu$$

$$B = (1 + r)(s_p - s_w)\omega_m \delta K, \text{ and}$$

$$Z = (B - A)^2 - 4(s_p r + s_w)(1 + r)\omega_m \delta K \cdot I\mu \qquad \text{in (e)},$$

$$= (A + B)^2 - 4s_p(1 + r)^2 \omega_m \delta K \cdot I\mu \qquad \text{in (d-1)}.$$[15]

Y, W, and P are obtained by using these solutions e and L and equations (6) to (7) and (1):

$$Y = e\mu L$$

$$= \frac{A + B \pm \sqrt{Z}}{2(1 + r)\delta K \cdot s_p} \times \frac{A - B \pm \sqrt{Z}}{2(s_p r + s_w)\omega_m \mu}, \tag{a-1}$$

$$W = \omega_m L$$

$$= \frac{A - B \pm \sqrt{Z}}{2(s_p r + s_w)\mu}, \text{ and} \tag{b-1}$$

$$P = Y - W$$

$$= \frac{\left(A - B \pm \sqrt{Z}\right)\left\{A - (1 + r)\omega_m \delta K(s_p + s_w + 2s_p r) \pm \sqrt{Z}\right\}}{4(s_p r + s_w)\mu \cdot (1 + r)\delta K \cdot s_p \omega_m}. \qquad \text{(c-1)}$$

Then ρ_c, ω, and π are obtained by using these (a-1), (b-1), (c-1), and identities (8), (9), and (10) in the section on "Model A: A Solution and Restraint Conditions."

$$\rho_c = \frac{A - (1 + r)\omega_m \delta K(s_p + s_w + 2s_p r) \pm \sqrt{Z}}{A + B \pm \sqrt{Z}}, \qquad \text{(8-2)}$$

$$\omega = \frac{2(1 + r)\delta K \cdot s_p \mu \omega_m}{\left(A + B \pm \sqrt{Z}\right)}, \text{ and} \qquad \text{(9-2)}$$

$$\pi = \frac{\left(A - B \pm \sqrt{Z}\right)\left\{A - (1 + r)\omega_m \delta K(s_p + s_w + 2s_p r) \pm \sqrt{Z}\right\}}{2(s_p r + s_w)\omega_m\left(A + B \pm \sqrt{Z}\right)K}, \qquad \text{(10-2)}$$

where $K_v = eK$ in identity (10).

By observation, here again, it is clear that both investment I and the money wage rate ω_m relate to ρ_c, ω, and π, respectively.

Restraint Conditions

Restraint conditions for Model B are almost the same as those of Model A. In addition to condition

$$1 \geq s_p > s_w \geq 0,$$

the model is subject to the following conditions:

i. The real wage rate is above a certain subsistence minimum level, and
ii. All variables are nonnegative.

The condition that a solution must be positive is found through the solving process. By observing a solution of L in (e), we consider the condition of $L > 0$. The denominator is positive, so the numerator becomes a question. Z must be positive in order to have a positive solution of $\sqrt{Z}$. Then we have

$$Z > 0. \qquad \text{(iia)}$$

If $Z > 0$, the condition of $L > 0$ is

$$A - B \pm \sqrt{Z} > 0.$$

Squaring both $(A - B)$ and $\sqrt{Z}$ and calculating the difference, we have

$$(A - B)^2 - (B - A)^2 + 4(s_p r + s_w)(1 + r)\omega_m \delta K \cdot I\mu$$
$$= 4(s_p r + s_w)(1 + r)\omega_m \delta K \cdot I\mu > 0 \quad \text{for} \quad A - B > 0.$$

Therefore, a necessary condition of $A - B \pm \sqrt{Z} > 0$ is

$$A - B > 0 \tag{iib}$$

(Refer to a solution of L and e for $A > 0$ and $B > 0$.) Observing ρ_c in (8-2),[16] the condition of $\rho_c > 0$ is

$$A - (1 + r)\omega_m \delta K(s_p + s_w + 2s_p r) > 0. \tag{iic}$$

We now have comparisons between these three conditions. Calculating (iib)–(iic), we have

$$2(1 + r)\omega_m \delta K(s_p r + s_w) > 0.$$

Hence condition (iib) is less restrictive than (iic), which means condition (iib) is satisfied if (iic) is fulfilled. Then comparing (iia) and (iic) by using reduced forms (see the previous footnote) results in (iia′) and (iic′) from (iia) and (iic), respectively:

$$Z = (B - A)^2 - 2AH > 0, \tag{iia}$$

$$\frac{(B - A)^2}{2A} > H \quad \text{for} \quad A > 0, \tag{iia′}$$

where

$$H = 2(1 + r)\omega_m \delta K(s_p r + s_w).$$

And

$$A - B - H > 0, \tag{iic}$$

$$A - B > H. \tag{iic′}$$

Calculating (iic′) – (iia′), we have

$$\frac{1}{2A}(A - B)(A + B) > 0, \qquad \text{for} \quad A > 0,\ B > 0, \quad \text{and} \quad A - B > 0.$$[17]

Condition (iic) is less restrictive than (iia), so if condition (iia) is fulfilled, conditions (iib) and (iic) are satisfied. We put (iia) as a restraint condition.

Model B: An Analysis in Comparative Statics

As with Model A, the effect of changes of I and ω_m on ρ_c, ω, and π, respectively, are examined. Because it is difficult to present simple equations, the analysis here proceeds in a more or less indirect way.

First, consider L and e. Under restraint condition (iia), we have in a plausible case (see Appendix 4E for the mathematical treatment):

$$\frac{\partial L}{\partial I} > 0, \quad \frac{\partial L}{\partial \omega_m} < 0, \tag{iiia}$$

and

$$\frac{\partial e}{\partial I} < 0, \quad \frac{\partial e}{\partial \omega_m} > 0. \tag{iiib}$$

These results concur with a general idea of a macroeconomy.

The Profit (Property) Share

Now consider ρ_c. Substituting (6) and (7) for Y and W in (1), respectively, and after some arrangements, we have

$$P = (e\mu - \omega_m)L. \tag{1'}$$

Substituting (1′) and (6) for P and Y in identity (8), we have

$$\rho_c \equiv \frac{P}{Y} = \frac{e\mu - \omega_m}{e\mu}, \tag{8a}$$

from which we derive the following growth-rate formula:

$$\hat{\rho}_c = \frac{\omega_m(\hat{e} - \hat{\omega}_m + \hat{\mu})}{e\mu - \omega_m}. \tag{8a'}$$

Replacing Y, W, and D in (4a) with (6), (7), and (11), respectively, and after some arrangements, we have

$$e\mu L = (1 + r)(\omega_m L + e \cdot \delta K)$$

$$e = \frac{R \cdot \omega_m L}{\mu L - R \cdot \delta K} \tag{d-2}$$

where

$$R = 1 + r,$$

from which we derive the growth-rate formula (assuming the change of productivity μ as well as money wage rate ω_m):[18]

$$\hat{e} = \hat{\omega}_m - \frac{R \cdot \delta K \hat{L} + \dot{\mu} L}{\mu L - R \cdot \delta K}. \tag{d-2'}$$

Then, replacing $(\hat{e} - \hat{\omega}_m)$ in (8a′) with $(\hat{e} - \hat{\omega}_m)$ gained from this (d-2′) and after some arrangements, we have

$$\hat{\rho}_c = -\frac{R \cdot \omega_m \delta K(\hat{\mu} + \hat{L})}{(e\mu - \omega_m)(\mu L - R \cdot \delta K)}. \tag{8a''}$$

If the growth rate of productivity is given as exogenous variable like that of money wage, the effect of μ on ρ_c is clear.[19] However, assume a productivity-employment function such as

$$\mu = c + hL \tag{5a}$$

where

$$\mu' > 0$$

(which is of similar but not identical type to equation (5) in Model A), from which is derived

$$\hat{\mu} = h\dot{L}/(c + hL). \tag{5a'}$$

In this case, when the labor force employed increases, productivity will increase. Productivity moves to the same direction as L. Therefore, the discussion on the change of L holds true for the change of μ.

Taking equation (8a″) and condition (iiia) above into consideration, it turns out that the increase of I has an upward effect on L and hence a downward effect on ρ_c, and the decrease of I has a downward effect on L and so an upward effect on ρ_c.

The Real Wage Rate

For the real wage rate ω, we have identity (9):

$$\omega \equiv \omega_m / e,$$

from which is derived a growth-rate equation

$$\hat{\omega} = \hat{\omega}_m - \hat{e}. \tag{9'}$$

Replacing the right side of this (9′) with $(\hat{\omega}_m - \hat{e})$ gained from (d-2′) results in

$$\hat{\omega} = \frac{R \cdot \delta K \hat{L} + \dot{\mu} L}{\mu L - R \cdot \delta K}. \tag{9''}$$

By equation (9″) and condition (iiia), an increase of I will have an upward effect on L and hence an upward effect on ω, and the decrease of I will have a downward effect on L and then on ω.

The Profit Rate

Finally, the profit rate π is given by identity (10):

$$\pi \equiv P/K_v.$$

Substituting (1′) and $K_v = eK$ for P and K_v in (10), we have

$$\pi = \frac{(e\mu - \omega_m)L}{eK}, \tag{10a}$$

from which is derived a growth-rate equation

$$\hat{\pi} = \frac{e\dot{\mu} + \omega_m(\hat{e} - \hat{\omega}_m)}{e\mu - \omega_m} + \hat{L}. \tag{10a'}$$

Then, replacing $(\hat{e} - \hat{\omega}_m)$ of the first part on the right side of (10a′) with $(\hat{e} - \hat{\omega}_m)$ obtained from (d-2′) and after some arrangements, results in

$$\hat{\pi} = \frac{\mu(e\mu L - \omega_m L - eR \cdot \delta K)(\hat{\mu} + \hat{L})}{(e\mu - \omega_m)(\mu L - R \cdot \delta K)}.\text{[20]} \tag{10a''}$$

By (10a″) and condition (iiia), an increase of I will have an upward effect on L and hence on π, and the decrease of I a downward effect on L and then on π.

By the solution of L, (d-2), and the respective growth-rate form including L, we have examined an effect of investment on ρ_c, ω, and π. The final relationship should be discussed as follows. First, given the relationship between the respective growth rate of I and ω_m, $\hat{L}$ is obtained by the growth-rate formula of L. Then, the result of L is applied to respective equations (8a″), (9″), and (10a″). This is an indirect explanation. For a more precise explanation, it may be necessary to discuss these matter directly by using the growth-rate formula gained from (8-2), (9-2), and (10-2), respectively. We have not presented these respective growth-rate equations. However, if the procyclical change of labor force employed L is robust, the respective result can be seen by feeding the change of L to (8a″), (9″), and (10a″). Therefore, the result holds true of the more precise explanation, though the explanation is indirect.

A Brief Summary: Concluding Remarks on Model B

1. This markup pricing equation applies Kaldor's model of income distribution to an underemployment economy in the short run. The price was set by adding a markup on the cost, *wages plus depreciation*. This is in line with Kaldor's approach in that (1) he does not take the marginal productivity theory, and (2) instead of it, he assumes oligopolistic behavior in the model—namely, he relates two restraint conditions for his model to oligopolistic behavior (see the restraint conditions (5) and (6) in Chapter 3).

2. The difference between Model B and Model 1976 is only whether capital K_v and then depreciation D were subject to the change of value or constant. This brought a difference in the solution of ρ_c, ω, and π. These solutions in Model B all include variables I and ω_m, but those in Model 1976 do not include ω_m. Furthermore, the solutions in Model B also all include variable μ, but in Model 1976 only e and ω include this; others (L, ρ_c, and π) do not.[21] However, it does not seem to bring a critical difference in the direction of change. The explanation here was indirect. Therefore, I am not sure how important the price change is in determining ρ_c, ω, and π due to the value change of D (and K_v). In fact, the share of D in GNP is various from country to country (it ranges from 1/7 (Japan) to 1/10).

3. For Model B, I tried to make the same kind of analysis as was made for Model A. An indirect approach was necessary because the solution (ρ_c, ω, and π) was complicated. The analysis showed that an increase of investment I tended to cause a decrease of the relative share of property ρ_c and an increase of both the real wage rate ω and the profit rate π. For a more precise explanation, taking a combined effect of I and ω_m into consideration, there might have some difference between the two models. For ρ_c, ω, and π are not independent from ω_m in Model B. However, assuming a procyclical change of L, the result would not basically change in the more precise analysis. In this respect Model B shares features with Model 1976.

4. The model has the possibility of explaining, more or less, the countercyclical change of the property share to the business cycle and the procyclical change of both the real wage rate and the profit rate. This model may have a weakness in explaining the procyclical movement of the property share to the business cycle. But the procyclical movement of the property share is not always a stylized fact. Furthermore, if a simple productivity-employment function (5a) is introduced to the model, this will give a direction of change in productivity in the business cycle—namely, a procyclical change in the case of without technical progress.

5. The workability of the model depends to a considerable degree on the markup pricing observed in a whole economy. Taking into consideration the existence of a competitive market (under free competition), to some extent this approach might be an oversimplification, at least in the sense of applying the model to the whole economy.

CONCLUSIONS: SOME REMARKS ON MODELS A AND B

Fundamental Characteristics of the Two Models

Fundamental characteristics of Models A and B are briefly summarized in the following outline.

First, investment was considered to be an independent variable—a strategic factor based on Kaldor's approach. Second, the volume of labor force employed is a function of investment in Model A (equation (4)). In Model B, instead of equation (4) a price-setting equation was introduced, which means that entrepreneurs set a price by marking up on *wages plus depreciation* at a customary rate (equation (4a)). Third, relating the economy to the operating rate in the industry, an underemployment economy was introduced as the case of an economy working at below the normal operation rate; that is the state of imperfect employment of capital.[22] Finally, labor productivity relates to this operation rate (equation (5) in Model A and (5a) in Model B).

Showing the process of the changes of important variables like a flow chart in the short run results in the following.

An Underemployment Economy

MODEL A. The increase of $I \rightarrow$ the increase of L

$\rightarrow$ { (i) The increase of operating rate in the industry, which causes the growth of productivity.
(ii) Growth of Y, W, and P.

$\rightarrow$ to effect on ρ_c, ω, and π.

The direction of growth of ρ_c ω, and π is determined by the growth relationship between investment and the money wage rate, respectively. The increase of I tends to cause the increase of ρ_c and π, and the decrease of I tends to cause the decrease of these values in Model A. Various cases for the growth rate of ω are possibilities.

MODEL B. But in Model B, the effect of I on ρ_c is opposite to that of Model A, though the effect of I on π is the same as in Model A. The effect of I on ω is positive. An indirect explanation was provided for these. The precise degrees of these results will be explained by respective growth-rate equations obtained from (8-2), (9-2), and (10-2).

Since nominal terms are used, Y, W, and P are not always downward even in the case of slump. Taking technical progress into consideration, it would be rare that the productivity decreases in absolute terms except for some phase in the slump.

A Full-Employment Economy

The amount of investment is large enough to sustain a full-employment economy, and the profit rate is also at a satisfactory level for entrepreneurs. If the investment/output ratio is stable and propensities to save (s_p and s_w) do not change, ρ_c, ω, and π would generally be constant. Taking technical progress[23] into consideration, ω would grow. This was the situation that Kaldor considered in the long run.

However, investment (then the investment/output ratio) will change in the short run, producing the following effect:

The increase of $I \rightarrow$ the increase of price $e \rightarrow \rho_c$ and π upward.

The change of the real wage rate depends on technical progress. The real wage rate would decrease if we do not consider technical progress and increase with technical progress.

With respect to the two alternative models, Model A possibly can be applied to this case, but there may be some difficulty in applying it to Model B. It is difficult to assume that a markup price is realized on a macrolevel as a whole in the full-employment economy, though entrepreneurs' (ex ante) pricing is applicable. In this situation the demand side often makes an overwhelming role. An oligopolistic or monopolistic rule is not always compatible with the full-employment economy.

Kaldor's original model is assumed to be basically applicable under full employment. I have argued his model and extended the discussion by introducing additional identities, making clear what the model explained (refer to Chapter 3, especially "Interpretation").

The Characteristics of the Model and the Validity

Which of these models is more effective in explaining the real economy? The validity of the employment-decision approach depends on how the volume of labor force employed is sensitive to the change of investment. The increase of investment, which is dealt with as an independent variable, tends to bring ρ_c and π upward.

The markup pricing approach holds true of the economy in which the price is adjusted in accordance with the change of the money wage rate—that is, an oligopolistic economy. Given I and ω_m, the volume of labor force employed is determined, and the entrepreneurs set a price based on markup pricing. The price would be realized.

Both approaches could explain some phases of the economy in the business cycle. The employment decision model (Model A) can explain, more or less, the countercyclical change of the labor share and the procyclical change of the profit rate to the business cycle. This model also explains the productivity change in the business cycle. The markup pricing model (Model B) can explain, more or less, the procyclical change of both the labor share and the profit rate to the business cycle, and some productivity change to it.

The validity of the employment-decision model as stated above, however, depends on how sensitive the volume of labor force employed is to the change of investment. This is a question of facts, though the fundamental relationship concurs with Dore's stylized facts.[24] A markup pricing model also has some weaknesses. It is true that some industries are oligopolistic and display markup pricing. However, for a whole economy, the extent of this price setting needs to be clarified. It is important to identify this in an aggregate economy. Another weakness of this approach was that it did not explain clearly the results of analysis like that in Model A.

Each model has its interpretative value and its weakness. The employment-decision model seems to explain more stylized facts than the markup pricing model. These weaknesses, more or less, relate to a question of facts. It is difficult to assess clearly the validity of these approaches on a highly abstract level. In this respect, perhaps we should leave assessment to the world of facts.

APPENDIX 4A: MODEL A: ON SOLUTION

We have output, wages, profits, and price level, respectively, as follows:

Output, *Y*

From equation (1), we have

$$P = Y - W. \tag{1'}$$

Substituting (1′) for P in (3), and furthermore this (3) for S in (2), we have

$$I = s_w W + s_p(Y - W).$$

By using (7), we have

$$I = s_w \omega_m L + s_p(Y - \omega_m L). \tag{2'}$$

Then, replacing L in (2′) with L in (4) and after some arrangements, we have

$$I = s_w \omega_m\{a + b(I - I^*)\} + s_p[Y - \omega_m\{a + b(I - I^*)\}]$$

$$s_p Y = I + (s_p - s_w)\omega_m\{a + b(I - I^*)\}$$

$$Y = \frac{I + (s_p - s_w)\omega_m\{a + b(I - I^*)\}}{s_p}.$$

Since the volume of employment L is determined simply by the volume of investment I (a, b, and I^* are given) by equation (4), we replace this L by X, then

$$Y = \frac{I + (s_p - s_w)\omega_m X}{s_p}, \tag{a}$$

where

$$X = a + b(I - I^*).$$

Wages, *W*

Substituting (4) for L in (7), we have

$$W = \omega_m L$$
$$= \omega_m X. \tag{b}$$

Profits, *P*

By substituting above (a) and (b) for Y and W in (1′) respectively, we have

$$P = \frac{I + (s_p - s_w)\omega_m X}{s_p} - \omega_m X$$
$$= \frac{I - s_w \omega_m X}{s_p}. \tag{c}$$

Price Level, *e*

We have e from (6):

$$e = \frac{Y}{\mu L}.$$

Substituting (a), (4), and (5) for this $Y/\mu L$, respectively, and after some arrangements, we have

$$e = \frac{I + (s_p - s_w)\omega_m X}{s_p\{c + h(X - L^*)\}X}. \tag{d}$$

APPENDIX 4B: EQUATIONS FOR COMPARATIVE STATICS

The Property Share, ρ_c

We put formula (8-1),

$$\rho_c = \frac{I - s_w \omega_m X}{I + (s_p - s_w)\omega_m X} = \frac{x}{x + y}, \tag{8-1}$$

where

$$x = I - s_w \omega_m X, \text{ and}$$
$$y = s_p \omega_m X.$$

We have a growth rate form of ρ_c from (8-1) above:

$$\hat{\rho}_c = \frac{y}{x + y}(\hat{x} - \hat{y}).$$

Here we calculate a growth rate of x and y, respectively:

$$x = I - s_w \omega_m X$$

$$\hat{x} = \frac{\{\dot{I} - (\hat{\omega}_m + \hat{X}) s_w \omega_m X\}}{I - s_w \omega_m X}, \text{ and}$$

$$y = s_p \omega_m X$$

$$\hat{y} = \hat{\omega}_m + \hat{X}.$$

Substituting these for x, $\hat{x}$, y, and $\hat{y}$ in the $\hat{\rho}_c$ form above, we have

$$\hat{\rho}_c = \frac{s_p \omega_m X}{I + (s_p - s_w)\omega_m X} \left[\frac{\{\dot{I} - (\hat{\omega}_m + \hat{X}) s_w \omega_m X\}}{I - s_w \omega_m X} - (\hat{\omega}_m + \hat{X}) \right].$$

After some arrangements we have the following in the above parentheses:

$$[\,] = \frac{1}{I - s_w \omega_m X} \{\dot{I} - I(\hat{\omega}_m + \hat{X})\}.$$

Regarding X, we have following equations:

$$X = a + b(I - I^*)$$

$$\hat{X} = \frac{b\dot{I}}{a + b(I - I^*)} = \frac{b\dot{I}}{X}$$

$$\dot{X} = b\dot{I}.$$

Therefore, putting these into [ ] above, we have

$$[\,] = \frac{1}{I - s_w \omega_m X} \left(\dot{I} - \frac{b\dot{I}I}{X} - I\hat{\omega}_m \right)$$

$$= \frac{I\{\hat{I}(X - bI) - \hat{\omega}_m X\}}{(I - s_w \omega_m X) X}.$$

Substituting this for the [ ] in $\hat{\rho}_c$ form above, we have

$$\hat{\rho}_c = \frac{s_p \omega_m I \{\hat{I}(X - bI) - \hat{\omega}_m X\}}{\{I + (s_p - s_w)\omega_m X\}(I - s_w \omega_m X)}. \tag{8-1'}$$

The Real Wage Rate, ω

We put equation (9-1)

$$\omega = \frac{s_p \omega_m \{c + h(X - L^*)\} X}{I + (s_p - s_w)\omega_m X} = \frac{y \cdot w}{I + z} \tag{9-1}$$

where

$$y = s_p \omega_m X,$$
$$w = c + h(X - L^*), \text{ and}$$
$$z = (s_p - s_w)\omega_m X.$$

From this we have a growth-rate form:

$$\hat{\omega} = \hat{y} + \hat{w} - \frac{\dot{I} + \dot{z}}{I + z}.$$

Here we calculate a growth rate of $y \cdot w$ and z, respectively:

$$y \cdot w = s_p \omega_m \{c + h(X - L^*)\} X$$
$$\hat{y} + \hat{w} = \hat{\omega}_m + \hat{X} + \frac{h\dot{X}}{c + h(X - L^*)}, \text{ and}$$
$$z = (s_p - s_w)\omega_m X$$
$$\dot{z} = (\hat{\omega}_m + \hat{X})(s_p - s_w)\omega_m X.$$

Substituting these $\hat{y}$, $\hat{w}$, and $\dot{z}$ for the respective one in the $\hat{\omega}$ form above, we have

$$\hat{\omega} = \hat{\omega}_m + \hat{X} + \frac{h\dot{X}}{c + h(X - L^*)} - \frac{\dot{I} + (\hat{\omega}_m + \hat{X})(s_p - s_w)\omega_m X}{I + (s_p - s_w)\omega_m X}$$
$$= \frac{1}{\{c + h(X - L^*)\}\{I + (s_p - s_w)\omega_m X\}} \times [I(\hat{\omega}_m + \hat{X})\{c + h(X - L^*)\}$$
$$+ h\dot{X}\{I + (s_p - s_w)\omega_m X\} - \dot{I}\{c + h(X - L^*)\}].$$

Dividing the numerator on the right side into two parts, we have, with regard to $\hat{\omega}_m$

$$\hat{\omega}_m I\{c + h(X - L^*)\},$$

and with regard to $\hat{X}$, $\dot{X}$ and $\dot{I}$,

$$(I\hat{X} - \dot{I})\{c + h(X - L^*)\} + h\dot{X}\{I + (s_p - s_w)\omega_m X\}.$$

As was shown above in "The Property Share,"

$$\hat{X} = \frac{b\dot{I}}{a + b(I - I^*)} = \frac{b\dot{I}}{X} \quad \text{and} \quad \dot{X} = b\dot{I}.$$

Then, we have for the latter part

$$\left(\frac{\dot{X}I}{X} - \dot{I}\right)\{c + h(X - L^*)\} + h\dot{X}\{I + (s_p - s_w)\omega_m X\}$$

$$= \left(\frac{b\dot{I}I}{X} - \dot{I}\right)\{c + h(X - L^*)\} + hb\dot{I}\{I + (s_p - s_w)\omega_m X\}$$

$$= \frac{\dot{I}}{X}[-(a - bI^*)\{c + h(X - L^*)\} + hbX\{I + (s_p - s_w)\omega_m X\}]$$

$$= \frac{\hat{I}I}{X}[-(a - bI^*)(c - hL^*) - hX(a - bI^*) + hbX\{I + (s_p - s_w)\omega_m X\}]$$

$$= \frac{\hat{I}I}{X}[\![-(a - bI^*)(c - hL^*) - hX[a - b\{I + I^* + (s_p - s_w)\omega_m X\}]]\!].$$ [25]

Substituting these results for the $\hat{\omega}$ form above, we have

$$\hat{\omega} = \frac{I}{\{c + h(X - L^*)\{I + (s_p - s_w)\omega_m X\}}\left[\!\!\left[-\frac{\hat{I}}{X}((a - bI^*) \times (c - hL^*) + hX[a - b\{I + I^* + (s_p - s_w)\omega_m X\}]) + \hat{\omega}_m\{c + h(X - L^*)\}\right]\!\!\right]. \tag{9-1'}$$

The Profit Rate, π

The profit rate formula (10-1) is

$$\pi = \frac{I - s_w\omega_m X}{s_p K_v}. \tag{10-1}$$

Here K_v is given and the numerator equals x above in "The Profit Share" (so the growth rate form of x is applicable). Then we have a growth-rate form:

$$\hat{\pi} = \frac{\dot{I} - (\hat{\omega}_m + \hat{X})s_w\omega_m X}{I - s_w\omega_m X}$$

$$= \frac{\dot{I} - b\dot{I}s_w\omega_m - \hat{\omega}_m s_w\omega_m X}{I - s_w\omega_m X}$$

$$= \frac{I\hat{I}(1 - bs_w\omega_m) - \hat{\omega}_m s_w\omega_m X}{I - s_w\omega_m X}. \tag{10-1'}$$

APPENDIX 4C: A MODEL (1976)

Model (1976)

Only part of the model is explained in the following. The 1976 model consists of the first six equations of Model B in this section:

$$Y \equiv W + P \tag{1}$$

$$I \equiv S \tag{2}$$

$$S \equiv s_w W + s_p P \tag{3}$$

$$Y = (1+ r)(W + D) \tag{4a}$$

$$Y \equiv e\mu L \tag{6}$$

$$W \equiv \omega_m L \tag{7}$$

The treatment of variables were almost the same as those in Model B. The relationship was articulated as follows:

1 independent variable	I
6 exogenous variables	s_w, s_p, r, μ, ω_m, and D
6 unknown variables	Y, W, P, S, e, and L
6 equations	(1) to (4a), (6) to (7)

Showing part of the solution of this model for discussion, it was

$$L = \frac{I - s_p(1 + r)D}{\omega_m(s_p r + s_w)}$$

$$e = \frac{\omega_m(1 + r)\{I - (s_p - s_w)D\}}{\mu\{I - s_p(1 + r)D\}}$$

$$\rho_c = \frac{Ir + s_w(1 + r)D}{(1 + r)\{I - (s_p - s_w)D\}}$$

$$\omega = \frac{\mu\{I - s_p(1 + r)D\}}{(1 + r)\{I - (s_p - s_w)D\}}$$

$$\pi = \frac{Ir + s_w(1 + r)D}{K_v(s_p r + s_w)}$$

By observation, it turns out that labor productivity μ has no direct relationship to the property share ρ_c and the profit rate π, but relates to the price level e and then to the real wage rate ω. These features are the same in Model A.

Then respective growth-rate forms of ρ_c, ω, and π for the comparative statics like that in Model A dealt with investment I and the money wage rate ω_m as strategic factors and with the others as given and constant:

$$\hat{\rho}_c = \frac{-\dot{I}(s_p r + s_w)D}{\{Ir + s_w(1 + r)D\}\{I - (s_p - s_w)D\}}$$

$$\hat{\omega} = \frac{\dot{I}(s_p r + s_w)D}{\{I - s_p(1 + r)D\}\{I - (s_p - s_w)D\}}$$

$$\hat{\pi} = \frac{\dot{I}r}{Ir + s_w(1 + r)D}.$$

Under the restraint conditions[26] of the model

$$I - s_p(1 + r)D > 0, \quad \text{and} \tag{A-ii}$$

$$I - (s_p - s_w)D > 0, \tag{A-ii$'$}$$

we had

$$\dot{I} \gtreqless 0 \quad \Rightarrow \quad \hat{\rho}_c \lesseqgtr 0, \quad \hat{\omega} \gtreqless 0, \quad \text{and} \quad \hat{\pi} \gtreqless 0.$$

When investment I increased, the relative share of property ρ_c would decrease, but the real wage rate ω and profit rate π increase. The changes of L and e were also discussed by using respective growth forms with respect to these ($\hat{L}$ and $\hat{e}$).

The above represents the model in summary, and a further expose can be found in Iyoda (1976) in detail. The model was not always presented in this style (in six articulated equations).

Other Kaleckian Models

The following two models are more comprehensive. However, we here limit our attention only to a couple of points, including their Kaleckian type equation.

A similar equation to (4a) is used by Watanabe (1979, ch. 8) in his extended model of income distribution in the short run.

When his function (8-5-10) is interpreted in terms of this chapter's notations,

$$e\mu L = (\omega_m L + e\delta K)(1 + r)$$

$$Y = (W + D)(1 + r)$$

where

ω_m and e = constants,
r = ex post markup rate (then not always customary constant), and
δ (the rate of depreciation) = 1.

In his model, ω_m and e are assumed as constants, then the real wage rate does not change. This is an unsatisfactory part of the model. However, one of the interesting points is that he divides the volume of employment into two parts, L' and L''. In the short run, L' changes in proportion to the change of output, assuming that average productivity of L' (= Y/L') is constant. But L'' is invariant to the change of output.

The model was a part of Watanabe's dissertation, "Economic Growth and Income Distribution: Micro Foundations of Macro Theory of Income Distribution," which was submitted to The University of Doshisha (Japan) in February 1978. However, his basic Kaleckian idea was seen in Watabnabe (1969), though the model was not satisfactory, particularly his price-setting equation.

Okamoto (1981, ch. 13) constructs a two-sector model in the short run as a synthesis of Keynesian and Kaleckian theories, incorporating a Kaleckian price-setting equation (his 9e) into model (notations are his own):

$$p_i = k_i c_i \qquad \text{(his 9e)}$$

where

p = price of goods,
k = the degree of monopoly, and
c = average prime cost.

Subscript i denotes a firm in consumer goods industries or investment goods industries.

This equation is a Kaleckian type of markup pricing. He assumes that productivity is constant until full capacity utilization of capital. Then he has

$$\frac{X_i}{N_i} = \bar{n}_i \qquad \text{(his 9b)}$$

where

X = output, and
N = employment.

These two functions (assumptions) fairly condition the result of his model, in particular in the underemployment economy.

APPENDIX 4D: MODEL B: ON SOLUTION

Labor force employed and price level are obtained as follows, respectively.

Labor Force Employed (L)

Substituting (6) and (7) for Y and W in (1), respectively, and after some arrangements, then

$$P = Y - W$$

$$= (e\mu - \omega_m)L. \tag{1''}$$

Replacing P in (3) with (1″), and then S in (2) with S obtained from (3), results in

$$I = s_w\omega_m L + s_p(e\mu - \omega_m)L$$

$$e\mu s_p L = I + (s_p - s_w)\omega_m L \tag{3'}$$

$$e = \frac{I + (s_p - s_w)\omega_m L}{\mu s_p L} \tag{3'-1}$$

Substituting (6), (7), and (11) for Y, W, and D in (4a), respectively, we have

$$e\mu L = (1 + r)(\omega_m L + e\delta K)$$

$$e\{\mu L - (1 + r)\delta K\} = (1 + r)\omega_m L \tag{3''}$$

$$e = \frac{(1 + r)\omega_m L}{\mu L - (1 + r)\delta K}. \tag{3''-1}$$

Then putting (3′-1) = (3″-1), we have

$$\frac{I + (s_p - s_w)\omega_m L}{\mu s_p L} = \frac{(1 + r)\omega_m L}{\mu L - (1 + r)\delta K}.$$

Making some arrangements, we have a quadratic equation with respect to L:

$$\mu s_p(1 + r)\omega_m L^2 = I\mu L - (1 + r)I\delta K + (s_p - s_w)\omega_m\mu L^2 - (1 + r)(s_p - s_w)\omega_m L \cdot \delta K$$

$$(s_p r + s_w)\omega_m\mu L^2 + \{(1 + r)(s_p - s_w)\omega_m\delta K - I\mu\}L + (1 + r)I\delta K = 0.$$

Solving this equation, we have

$$L = \frac{A - B \pm \sqrt{Z}}{2(s_p r + s_w)\omega_m\mu}, \tag{e}$$

where

$A = I\mu$,
$B = (1 + r)(s_p - s_w)\omega_m\delta K$, and
$Z = (B - A)^2 - 4(s_p r + s_w)(1 + r)\omega_m\delta K \cdot I\mu$.

Price Level (e)

Take L from (3′) and (3″), respectively;

$$L\{s_p \cdot e\mu - (s_p - s_w)\omega_m\} = I$$

$$L = \frac{I}{s_p \cdot e\mu - (s_p - s_w)\omega_m} \qquad (3'\text{-}2)$$

and

$$L\{e\mu - (1 + r)\omega_m\} = (1 + r)e\delta K$$

$$L = \frac{(1 + r)e\delta K}{e\mu - (1 + r)\omega_m}. \qquad (3''\text{-}2)$$

Putting (3′-2) = (3″-2), we have

$$\frac{I}{s_p \cdot e\mu - (s_p - s_w)\omega_m} = \frac{(1 + r)e\delta K}{e\mu - (1 + r)\omega_m}.$$

Making some arrangements, we have a quadratic equation with respect to e:

$$Ie\mu - I(1 + r)\omega_m = (1 + r)e^2 s_p\mu \cdot \delta K - (1 + r)(s_p - s_w)e\omega_m \cdot \delta K$$
$$(1 + r)\delta K \cdot s_p\mu e^2 - \{(1 + r)(s_p - s_w)\omega_m \cdot \delta K + I\mu\}e + I(1 + r)\omega_m = 0.$$

Solving this equation, we have

$$e = \frac{A + B \pm \sqrt{Z}}{2(1 + r)\delta K \cdot s_p\mu}, \qquad (\text{d-1})$$

where

$$Z = (A + B)^2 - 4s_p(1 + r)^2\omega_m\delta K \cdot I\mu.$$

(See note 15 on "Z in (e) = Z in (d-1)").

APPENDIX 4E: THE FIRST PARTIAL DERIVATIVE AND GROWTH-RATE EQUATIONS

The First Partial Derivative

Regarding $\partial L/\partial I$ and $\partial L/\partial \omega_m$

A quadratic equation with respect to L in Appendix 4D is

$$(s_p r + s_w)\omega_m \cdot \mu L^2 + \{(1 + r)(s_p - s_w)\omega_m \cdot \delta K - I\mu\}L + (1 + r)\delta K \cdot I = 0,$$

from which we have the first partial derivative of L with respect to I:

$$\{2(s_p r + s_w)\omega_m \cdot \mu L + (1 + r)(s_p - s_w)\omega_m \cdot \delta K - I\mu\}\partial L - \{\mu L - (1 + r)\delta K\}\partial I = 0.$$

Then,

$$\frac{\partial L}{\partial I} = \frac{\mu L - (1 + r)\delta K}{2(s_p r + s_w)\omega_m \cdot \mu L + (1 + r)(s_p - s_w)\omega_m \cdot \delta K - I\mu}.$$

Considering equations (6) and (4a), the numerator is

$$\begin{aligned} \mu L - (1 + r)\delta K &= (1/e)\{Y - (1 + r)D\} \\ &= (1/e)(1 + r)W > 0. \end{aligned}$$

Profits P are obtained by equations (1) and (4a):

$$P = r(W + D) + D. \tag{f}$$

Then, investment is derived from equations (2), (3), and (f):

$$\begin{aligned} I &= s_w W + s_p P \\ &= s_w W + s_p\{r(W + D) + D\}. \end{aligned} \tag{2a}$$

Substituting this for I in the denominator and using equations (6), (7), and (11), then

$$\begin{aligned} &2(s_p r + s_w)\omega_m \cdot \mu L + (1 + r)(s_p - s_w)\omega_m \cdot \delta K - I\mu \\ &= 2(s_p r + s_w)\omega_m \cdot \mu L + (1 + r)(s_p - s_w)\omega_m \cdot \delta K - \{s_w W + s_p r(W + D) + s_p D\}\mu \\ &= \mu\{2(s_p r + s_w)W - s_w W - s_p r(W + D) - s_p D\} + (1 + r)(s_p - s_w)\omega_m \cdot \delta K \\ &= \mu\{(s_p r + s_w)W - s_p(1 + r)D\} + (1 + r)(s_p - s_w)\omega_m \cdot \delta K \\ &= \mu\{(s_p rW - s_p(1 + r)D\} + s_p(1 + r)\omega_m \cdot \delta K + \mu \cdot s_w W - s_w(1 + r)\omega_m \cdot \delta K \\ &= (1/eL)\,[s_p\{Yr \cdot W - Y(1 + r)D + (1 + r)W \cdot D\} + s_w\{Y \cdot W - (1 + r)W \cdot D\}] \\ &= (1/eL)\,[s_p\{Yr \cdot W - (1 + r)D(Y - W)\} + s_w W\{Y - (1 + r)D\}]. \end{aligned}$$

From equations (1) and (4a),

$$\frac{W}{eL}\left[s_p\left\{Yr - (1 + r)\frac{D}{W} \cdot P\right\} + s_w(1 + r)W\right].$$

If the section in { } above is positive,

$$Yr - (1 + r)\frac{D}{W} \cdot P > 0.$$

Then

$$\frac{r}{1 + r} > \frac{D}{W} \cdot \frac{P}{Y}. \tag{iv}$$

Putting expected maximum values for D/W and P/Y,

$$\frac{D}{W} = 0.30 \quad \text{and} \quad \frac{P}{Y} = 0.45,$$

results in

$$\frac{r}{1+r} > \left(\frac{30}{100}\right) \cdot \left(\frac{45}{100}\right)$$

$$r > \frac{27}{173} \doteqdot 0.156$$

This means that, if markup rate r is greater than 0.156, condition (iv) is fulfilled in this case. r in general is considered to be greater than this value. We consider condition (iv) is plausible, so the denominator is positive. Then

$$\frac{\partial L}{\partial I} > 0.$$

For $\partial L/\partial \omega_m$, we have from the quadratic equation with respect to L

$$\{2(s_p r + s_w)\omega_m \cdot \mu L + (1 + r)(s_p - s_w)\omega_m \cdot \delta K - I\mu\}\partial L + \{(s_p r + s_w)\mu L^2 + (1 + r)(s_p - s_w)\delta K \cdot L\}\partial \omega_m = 0.$$

Then

$$\frac{\partial L}{\partial \omega_m} = \frac{-\{(s_p r + s_w)\mu L^2 + (1 + r)(s_p - s_w)\delta K \cdot L\}}{2(s_p r + s_w)\omega_m \cdot \mu L + (1 + r)(s_p - s_w)\omega_m \cdot \delta K - I\mu}.$$

From this we have

Numerator < 0 for $s_p - s_w > 0$, and

Denominator > 0 for $\dfrac{r}{1+r} > \dfrac{D}{W} \cdot \dfrac{P}{Y}$.

Therefore,

$$\frac{\partial L}{\partial \omega_m} < 0.$$

Regarding $\partial e/\partial I$ and $\partial e/\partial \omega_m$

A quadratic equation with respect to e in Appendix 4D is

$$(1 + r)\delta K \cdot s_p \mu e^2 - \{(1 + r)(s_p - s_w)\omega_m \cdot \delta K + I\mu\}e + I(1 + r)\omega_m = 0,$$

from which we have the first partial derivative of e with respect to I:

$$[2(1+r)\delta K \cdot s_p \mu e - \{(1+r)(s_p - s_w)\omega_m \cdot \delta K + I\mu\}]\partial e + \{(1+r)\omega_m - e\mu\}\partial I = 0.$$

Then

$$\frac{\partial e}{\partial I} = \frac{e\mu - (1+r)\omega_m}{2(1+r)\delta K \cdot s_p \mu e - \{(1+r)(s_p - s_w)\omega_m \cdot \delta K + I\mu\}}.$$

Considering equations (6) and (4a), the numerator is

$$\begin{aligned}
& e\mu - (1+r)\omega_m \\
&= (1/L)\{e\mu L - (1+r)\omega_m L\} \\
&= (1/L)\{Y - (1+r)W\} \\
&= (1/L)(1+r)D > 0.
\end{aligned}$$

Replacing I in the denominator with that of (2a) and using equations (6), (7), and (11), we have

$$\begin{aligned}
& 2(1+r)\delta K \cdot s_p \mu e - \{(1+r)(s_p - s_w)\omega_m \cdot \delta K + I\mu\} \\
&= (1/eL)\{2(1+r)s_p D \cdot Y - (1+r)(s_p - s_w)W \cdot D - IY\} \\
&= (1/eL)[2(1+r)s_p D \cdot Y - (1+r)(s_p - s_w)W \cdot D - \{s_w W + s_p r(W+D) + s_p D\}Y] \\
&= (1/eL)[\{2s_p(1+r)D - s_w W - s_p r(W+D) - s_p D\}Y - (1+r)(s_p - s_w)W \cdot D] \\
&= (1/eL)[\{s_p(1+r)D - (s_w + s_p r)W\}Y - (1+r)(s_p - s_w)W \cdot D] \\
&= \frac{W}{eL}\left[\left\{s_p(1+r)\frac{D}{W} \cdot Y - (s_w + s_p r)Y - (1+r)(s_p - s_w)D\right\}\right] \\
&= \frac{W}{eL}\left[\left\{s_p(1+r)\frac{D}{W}(Y - W) - (s_w + s_p r)Y + s_w(1+r))D\right\}\right].
\end{aligned}$$

Considering equations (1) and (4a), we have

$$\begin{aligned}
& \frac{W}{eL}\left[s_p\left\{(1+r)\frac{D}{W} \cdot P - Yr\right\} - s_w\{Y - (1+r)D\}\right] \\
&= \frac{W}{eL}\left[s_p\left\{(1+r)\frac{D}{W} \cdot P - Yr\right\} - s_w(1+r)W\right] \\
&= \frac{-W}{eL}\left[s_p\left\{Yr - (1+r)\frac{D}{W} \cdot P\right\} + s_w(1+r)W\right].
\end{aligned}$$

The section in [ ] is the same as that of denominator in $\partial L/\partial I$. Then we have[27]

Numerator > 0, and

$$\text{Denominator} < 0 \quad \text{for} \quad \frac{r}{1+r} > \frac{D}{W} \cdot \frac{P}{Y}.$$

Therefore,

$$\frac{\partial e}{\partial I} < 0.$$

For $\partial e/\partial \omega_m$, we have from the quadratic equation with respect to e

$$[2(1+r)\delta K \cdot s_p \mu e - \{(1+r)(s_p - s_w)\omega_m \cdot \delta K + I\mu\}]\partial e - \{(1+r)(s_p - s_w)e\delta K - I(1+r)\}\partial \omega_m = 0.$$

Then

$$\frac{\partial e}{\partial \omega_m} = \frac{(1+r)(s_p - s_w)e\delta K - I(1+r)}{2(1+r)\delta K \cdot s_p \mu e - \{(1+r)(s_p - s_w)\omega_m \cdot \delta K + I\mu\}}.$$

Using equation (11), the numerator is

$$(1+r)(s_p - s_w)e\delta K - I(1+r) = (1+r)\{(s_p - s_w)D - I\} < 0 \quad \text{for} \quad (s_p - s_w)D - I < 0.$$

$(s_p - s_w)D - I < 0$ is clear, for it deals with I in the gross term, which includes depreciation D. Under condition (iv), the denominator is negative. Then

$$\frac{\partial e}{\partial \omega_m} > 0.$$

Growth Rate Equations

We here obtain growth-rate equations of the price e, the property share ρ_c, and the profit rate π. Related solutions in the text are as follows:

$$\rho_c = \frac{e\mu - \omega_m}{e\mu} \tag{8a}$$

$$e = \frac{R\omega_m L}{\mu L - R \cdot \delta K} \tag{d-2}$$

$$\pi = \frac{(e\mu - \omega_m)L}{eK} \tag{10a}$$

We derive a growth rate formula of e from (d-2):

$$\hat{e} = \hat{\omega}_m + \hat{L} - \frac{\dot{\mu}L + \mu\dot{L}}{\mu L - R \cdot \delta K}$$
$$= \hat{\omega}_m - \frac{R \cdot \delta K\hat{L} + \dot{\mu}L}{\mu L - R \cdot \delta K}. \tag{d-2'}$$

From (8a) we derive a growth rate formula of ρ_c:

$$\hat{\rho}_c = \frac{\dot{e}\mu + e\dot{\mu} - \dot{\omega}_m}{e\mu - \omega_m} - (\hat{e} + \hat{\mu})$$
$$= \frac{\omega_m(\hat{e} - \hat{\omega}_m + \hat{\mu})}{e\mu - \omega_m}. \tag{8a'}$$

Then, replacing $(\hat{e} - \hat{\omega}_m)$ in (8a′) with $(\hat{e} - \hat{\omega}_m)$ gained from (d-2′), we have

$$\hat{\rho}_c = \frac{\omega_m}{e\mu - \omega_m} \cdot \left(\hat{\mu} - \frac{R \cdot \delta K\hat{L} + \dot{\mu}L}{\mu L - R \cdot \delta K}\right)$$
$$= \frac{-R\omega_m \cdot \delta K(\hat{\mu} + \hat{L})}{(e\mu - \omega_m)(\mu L - R \cdot \delta K)}. \tag{8a''}$$

The growth-rate formula of the profit rate π is gained from (10a):

$$\hat{\pi} = \frac{(\dot{e}\mu + e\dot{\mu} - \dot{\omega}_m)}{e\mu - \omega_m} + \hat{L} - \hat{e}$$
$$= \frac{e\dot{\mu} + \omega_m(\hat{e} - \hat{\omega}_m)}{e\mu - \omega_m} + \hat{L}. \tag{10a'}$$

Then, replacing $(\hat{e} - \hat{\omega}_m)$ of the first part on the right side of (10a′) with $(\hat{e} - \hat{\omega}_m)$ obtained from (d-2′), we have

$$\hat{\pi} = \frac{1}{e\mu - \omega_m}\left\{e\dot{\mu} + \omega_m\left(-\frac{R \cdot \delta K\hat{L} + \dot{\mu}L}{\mu L - R \cdot \delta K}\right) + \hat{L}(e\mu - \omega_m)\right\}$$
$$= \frac{1}{e\mu - \omega_m}\left\{\frac{\dot{\mu}(e\mu L - \omega_m L - eR \cdot \delta K) + \hat{L}\mu(e\mu L - \omega_m L - eR \cdot \delta K)}{\mu L - R \cdot \delta K}\right\}$$
$$= \frac{\mu(e\mu L - \omega_m L - eR \cdot \delta K)(\hat{\mu} + \hat{L})}{(e\mu - \omega_m)(\mu L - R \cdot \delta K)}. \tag{10a''}$$

NOTES

1. Sen (1963) makes not only fine development in this direction but also an interesting comparison between neoclassical and neo-Keynesian theories of distribution. He classifies theories of distribution into four systems (or models): (1) the neoclassical system (Solow, 1956; Swan, 1956;

Meade, 1960), (2) the neo-Keynesian system (Kaldor, 1955–1956, 1961; Robinson, 1953–1954, 1956, 1960b), (3) the Johansen model (Johansen, 1960), and (4) the general theory model.

Sen himself presents three types of model: Model I (full employment; fixed investment in real terms), Model II (full employment; fixed investment in money terms), and Model III (underemployment). He argues that system (1), (2) and (3) above are explained in Model I or Model II. These three are constructed using some restrictive assumptions to obtain their special results. Model III is the general theory model, which includes the first postulate of the neoclassical and Keynesian hypothesis (which treats investment as an independent variable). He says that this model "indicates how Keynes could offer all the results of N.K. [neo-Keynesian] model, barring the condition of full employment, without encountering any contradictions" (Sen, 1963, p. 64).

2. My assumptions (iv) and (v) are supported by the following stylized facts in the business cycle (Dore, 1993, pp. 20–22): an *anticyclical unemployment rate* (which is included in his stylized fact 1), a procyclycal relationship between labor productivity and output (fact 6), and procyclical nature of investment in fixed capital and inventories (fact 8).

My assumption iv has a close relationship to procyclical nature of investment and the anticyclical unemployment rate. It is possible to derive this assumption from these two stylized facts. Assumption v corresponds to the procyclical relationship between labor productivity and output and the procyclical nature of investment.

3. The notations are rather conventional and here not specified further. Because this model attempts to deal with the whole economy, output can be GDP, GNP, or NI (national income). Other totals (categories) such as investment and savings are properly specified in accordance with the output total taken for the estimate of the actual economy.

4. An economy without technical progress is subject to diminishing returns for $L_{fk} < L < L_{fl}$. Then the labor productivity μ will decrease, and there is no reason why more workers are employed. However, in an actual economy the workforce employed increases until the peak of the business cycle, and that productivity also grows until that time (see productivity Figures 2.8a, 2.9a, and 2.10a in Chapter 2; the only exception was 1979 in the United States during our observation period).

Taking the above into consideration, we should compute a quadratic equation for $L_{fk} < L < L_{fl}$, which has the following features:

$\mu' < 0$ without technical progress, and

$\mu' \geq 0$ or $\mu' < 0$ with technical progress.

The difference between L_{fk} and L_{fl} varies from country to country and time to time. It seems that "the greater is the difference, the larger the unemployment rate is."

5. For mathematical treatments in detail, see Appendix 4A to this chpater.

6. This condition is the same kind as Kaldor's (4), which indirectly shows the upper limit of investment (and directly the upper limit of ρ_c) under the full-employment economy. In this sense, it is not necessary to keep this condition. However, if it is understood in its broader sense, it might be necessary to include it. For a subsistence minimum level is historical and social, defined in a relative sense. It may be considered as a level at which trade unions desperately resist the pressure toward the decrease of the real wage rate.

7. See Appendix 4B for mathematical treatments in detail.

8. Consider $X - bI > 0$. We can rewrite this as follows:

$$
\begin{aligned}
X - bI &= a + b(I - I^*) - bI \\
&= a - bI^*
\end{aligned}
$$

This is the case that $I = 0$ in equation (4). Even in this case, L cannot be zero. So it must be $a - bI^* > 0$. b is an extremely tiny figure in contrast with a. $X/(X - bI)$ exceeds one but only by very small margin. Then ρ_c would turn to positive at a fairly small ratio of $\hat{I}$ to $\hat{\omega}_m$.

9. Concerning V, $c - hL^*$ in the first term of V is the extreme case that the labor force employed L is zero in equation (5), which never happens in the economy. Then $\mu = c - hL^* = 0$. So whether V is positive or not depends on the second term. By using (a) $Y = \{I + (s_p - s_w)\omega_m X\}/s_p$, the section in [ ] in the second term of V is expressed as

$$[\ ] = a - b\{I + I^* + (s_p - s_w)\omega_m X\}$$
$$= a - b(I^* + s_p Y).$$

Suppose the extreme case that $L = 0$ if $I = -K_\nu$, which means scrapping all capital stock. Then we have

$$L = a + b(-K_\nu - I^*) = 0.$$

Calculating [ ] – L above, we have $-bs_p Y + bK_\nu$. From this, we have:

If $(K_\nu\ /\ Y) > s_p$, section in [ ] > 0, hence $V > 0$.

It may be plausible to consider V positive. However, it is hard to explain it logically at the moment. We have also showed the negative case ($V < 0$).

10. We can explain $(1 - bs_w\omega_m) > 0$ from restraint condition (i) $(I - s_w\omega_m X > 0)$. We can rewrite this as follows:

$$I - s_w\omega_m X$$
$$= I - s_w\omega_m\{a + b(I - I^*)\}$$
$$= I - bIs_w\omega_m - s_w\omega_m(a - bI^*)$$
$$= I(1 - bs_w\omega_m) - s_w\omega_m(a - bI^*).$$

We consider $a - bI^* > 0$ (see note 8 of this chapater). When $I - s_w\omega_m X > 0$ is satisfied, $I(1 - bs_w\omega_m)$ must be positive and larger than $s_w\omega_m(a - bI^*)$, which is also positive. Then it is clear that

$$1 - bs_w\omega_m > 0.$$

11. By using equations (2) and (3), we can rewrite the denominator as follows:

$$I - bIs_w\omega_m$$
$$= s_w W + s_p P - bIs_w\omega_m$$
$$= s_p P + s_w\omega_m L - bIs_w\omega_m$$
$$= s_p P + s_w\omega_m(L - bI).$$

12. This equation (4a) may be called a Kaleckian type. See the model in Appendix 4C. In Japan, for example, Watanabe (1979) and Okamoto (1981) also present comprehensive models in the short run by incorporating their Kaleckian type equations into them, respectively. We shall make a short remark on these in Appendix 4C.

13. This is almost the same as the model the writer presented (Iyoda, 1976, p. 58 n. 5), where K denotes the volume of capital.

14. See Appendix 4D for the mathematical treatment.

15. If we calculate

$$(B - A)^2 - 4(s_p r + s_w)(1 + r)\omega_m\delta K \cdot I\mu$$

in the root of solution L, and

$$(A + B)^2 - 4s_p(1 + r)^2 \omega_m \delta K \cdot I\mu$$

in the root of solution e respectively, both become the same as

$$A\{A - 2\omega_m \delta K(1 + r)(s_p + s_w + 2s_p r)\} + \{(1 + r) \times (s_p - s_w)\omega_m \delta K\}.$$

16. We can rewrite the numerator of (8-2) as follows:

$$A - (1 + r)\omega_m \delta K(s_p + s_w + 2s_p r) \pm \sqrt{Z}$$

$$= A - (1 + r)\omega_m \delta K(s_p + s_w + 2s_p r) \pm \sqrt{(B - A)^2 - 4(s_p r + s_w)(1 + r)\omega_m \delta K \cdot I\mu}$$

$$= A - B - H \pm \sqrt{(B - A)^2 - 2AH}$$

where

$$H = 2(1 + r)\,\omega_m \delta K(s_p r + s_w).$$

By using this reduced form, we have a comparison between

$$(A - B - H) \quad \text{and} \quad \sqrt{(B - A)^2 - 2AH}.$$

Calculating a square of each and then the difference, we have

$$\{(A - B) - H\}^2 - \{(B - A)^2 - 2AH\}$$
$$= H(2B + H) > 0, \qquad \text{for } A > 0,\ B > 0,\ H > 0, \text{ and } A - B - H > 0.$$

It turns out

$$A - (1 + r)\omega_m \delta K(s_p + s_w + 2s_p r) > \sqrt{Z},$$

and then the condition of $\rho_c > 0$ becomes (iic).

17. We have

$$A - B - \frac{(B - A)^2}{2A}$$

$$= \frac{1}{2A}\{2A(A - B) - (B^2 + A^2 - 2AB)\}$$

$$= \frac{1}{2A}(A^2 - B^2)$$

$$= \frac{1}{2A}(A - B)(A + B) > 0, \qquad \text{for} \quad A > 0,\ B > 0, \text{ and } A - B > 0.$$

The writer thanks Professor Robert Daniel for this verification.

18. See Appendix 4E for mathematical treatments of growth-rate formulas $\hat{e}$ of (d-2′), $\hat{\rho}_c$ of (8a″), and $\hat{\pi}$ of (10a″).

19. If productivity is constant, we have a form by putting $\hat{\mu} = 0$ in (8a″). The stylized facts in Chapter 2 show that productivity is not constant. Refer to Figures 2.8a, 2.9a, and 2.10a in Chapter 2.

20. The section in parentheses of the numerator in (10a″) is positive. Reducing each factor into simple form results in

$$\begin{aligned}(\ ) &= e\mu L - \omega_m L - eR \cdot \delta K \\ &= Y - W - (1 + r)D.\end{aligned}$$

Substituting equation (4a) for Y in ( ) above results in

$$(\ ) = rW > 0.$$

21. See Appendix 4C. ρ_c, ω, and π in Model 1976 have no relationship with ω_m. So it is easy to have respective growth-rate forms and to find a clear-cut effect of I on these variables.

22. Arguments were focused on the degree of employment of capital. In an actual situation, full employment of capital can exist with underemployment of the labor force, due to some market friction or institutional factors. This kind of unemployment is called *frictional* or *structural* unemployment.

23. For Kaldor seems to assume that the technical progress is a Harrod's neutral type, which keeps the K/Y constant in the long run.

24. Refer to previous note 2 of this Chapter.

25. Putting back X into original form in

$$\frac{b\dot{I}I}{X} - \dot{I} = \frac{\dot{I}}{X}\left(bI - X\right),$$

and after some arrangements, we have

$$\begin{aligned}bI - X &= bI - \{a + b(I - I^*)\} \\ &= -(a - bI^*).\end{aligned}$$

26. Calculating (A-ii) − (A-ii′), we have

$$-(s_p r + s_w) D < 0.$$

Hence, condition (A-ii′) is less restrictive than (A-ii), which means that condition (A-ii′) is satisfied if (A-ii) is fulfilled.

Condition (A-ii) is plausible. Here investment is defined in terms of gross. Supposing a special case in which $s_p = 1$, then

$$I > (1 + r)D.$$

This means that if investment is greater than D plus profit margins on D, the condition is satisfied. In a more general case of $s_p < 1$, the condition is less restrictive than the special case because of $s_p(1 + r)D < (1 + r)D$.

27. The result is proved as follows. Adding both denominators (of $\partial L/\partial I$ and $\partial e/\partial I$), we have

$$\begin{aligned}&2(s_p r + s_w)\omega_m \cdot \mu L + 2(1 + r)\delta K \cdot s_p \mu e - 2I\mu \\ &= 2\mu\{(s_p r + s_w)W + s_p(1 + r)D - I\} \\ &= 2\mu\{(s_w W + s_p r(W + D) + s_p D - I\} \\ &= 0. \qquad \text{(consider (2a))}\end{aligned}$$

5. OTHER MODELS

Two broad types of models have been used to explain the business cycle. One type is the neoclassical model based on the Walrasian system, which emphasizes the optimization of private economic actors. The other is a Keynesian type, which, for understanding economic fluctuations, requires not just an understanding of the intricacies of general equilibrium but also an appreciation of the possibility of market failure on a grand scale.

The precise distinction between these two types is hard to make. After World War II, economists were more or less Keynesians with their feet in neoclassical economics. Nicholas Kaldor, in the tradition of Cambridge Keynesians, did not consider profit-maximizing principles in his macroeconomic theory of income distribution.

However, during the past decade or so, each school has seen new development in its fundamental approach. On the one hand, there is the real business cycle (RBC) theory, which is the latest incarnation of the classical view of economic fluctuations. On the other hand, there is the new Keynesian theory. These two theories are discussed in this chapter as representative theories emanating from each school. First RBC theory is examined, then new Keynesian theory, and finally some tentative conclusions are made.

THE REAL BUSINESS CYCLE THEORY

Introduction

Charles I. Plosser's "Understanding Real Business Cycles" (1989) is representative of the RBC approach. In his examination of the flaws of Keynesian economics, he argues that the essential flaw in the Keynesian interpretation of macroeconomic phenomenon was the absence of a consistent foundation based on the "choice-theoretic framework" of microeconomics.[1] The absence of an underlying choice-theoretic framework also plagued the dynamic elements of Keynesian models. Plosser argues that the foundations of the Keynesian model were static and oriented toward the short run. Dynamic elements were introduced through accelerator mechanisms and later in the form of price- or wage-adjustment equations and partial adjustment models of one form or another. These dynamic specifications, however, did not arise from any choice-theoretic framework of maximization but were simply behavioral rules that characterized either agents or, more frequently, markets in general.

Plosser emphasizes that, in order to understand the business cycle, it is important and necessary to understand the characteristics of a "perfectly working dynamic system." Hicks (1933, p. 32) makes this point quite clearly, arguing that "the idealized state of dynamic equilibrium . . . give[s] as a way of assessing the extent or degree of disequilibrium." In 1939, Hicks set out the basic elements and tools for determining the character of the "idealized state" in more detail in *Value and Capital*. Progress toward understanding this idealized state is essential because it is logically impossible to attribute an important portion of fluctuations to market failure without this understanding. Fortunately, in the last decade economists (including Lucas, 1980) have developed the analytical tools to follow through with the Hicks program.

Therefore, RBC models take the first necessary steps in evaluating and understanding Hicks's "idealized state of dynamic equilibrium." Consequently, these models must be at the core of any understanding economists will provide of business cycles.

The Models

The Basic RBC Framework

THE NEOCLASSICAL MODEL OF CAPITAL ACCUMULATION. RBC models[2] consider the neoclassical model of capital accumulation as the benchmark model for understanding economic fluctuations as well as growth. They view aggregate economic variables as the outcome of the decision made by many individual agents acting to maximize their utility subject to production possibilities and resource constraints.

The economic environment is an economy populated by many "identical agents" (households) that live forever:

- The utility of each agent is some function of the consumption and leisure they expect to enjoy over their lifetimes;
- Each agent is also treated as having access to a constant returns to scale production technology for the single commodity in this economy;
- The production technology is assumed to be subject to temporary productivity shifts or technological changes that provide the underlying source of variation in the economic environment to which agents must respond; and
- For simplicity, they assume that these shifts, past and future, are known with certainty to all agents and thus agents have perfect foresight.

The model is clearly simple and unrealistic but, at this point, only provides a benchmark of the features of a dynamic market equilibrium. It is a purely real model, driven by technology or productivity disturbances, and hence, following Long and Plosser (1983), it has been labeled a *real business cycle model.*

EQUILIBRIUM OUTCOMES. Plosser interprets utility-maximizing choices of consumption, investment, and work effort by Robinson Crusoe as the per capita outcomes of a competitive market economy. In the absence of productivity disturbances, these Robinson Crusoe optimum choices will, under a broad set of conditions, converge to constants or steady-state values.[3]

RESPONSES TO PRODUCTIVITY DISTURBANCES. A productivity disturbance, if it is long-lived or persistent, results in a dynamic response by Robinson Crusoe that involves variations in output, work effort, consumption, and investment over many periods. There are no market failures in the economy, so Robinson Crusoe's response to the productivity shifts are optimal, and the economy is Pareto efficient at all points in time.

SUPPLY AND DEMAND. Although it is common to refer to these RBC models as models that are driven by aggregate "supply shocks," there is nothing inherent in the business-cycle model that limits it to the analysis of variations in technology or supply. Shocks occur to either preferences, technologies and opportunities, or resources and endowments. Each type of shock will generally affect both the supply and demand schedules in a particular market.

STOCHASTIC MODELS AND UNCERTAINTY. The model deals with the certainty case, but it can be adapted to handle uncertainty. In that case, the resulting set of time paths for consumption, work effort, and capital are then a linear rational expectations equilibrium rather than a perfect foresight equilibrium.

Economic Growth and Business Cycles

The neoclassical model of capital accumulation predicts that per capita values of output, capital, and consumption will, in the absence of disturbances to productivity, converge to constants or steady-state values. But the basic neoclassical model does not offer an explanation of this sustained growth in per capita values.

TECHNOLOGICAL CHANGE. In a classic paper, Solow (1957) argued that technical change, in addition to the capital per worker, was an important source of variation in output per capita. Solow constructed estimates of U.S. technological change using data from 1909 to 1949. At least since Solow's seminal work, it has been common to think of economic growth as something that can be studied independently of economic fluctuations. In fact, the use of the phrase *growth theory* was an intentional attempt to distinguish it from a theory of the business cycle. As stressed by Hicks (1965), however, there is no compelling economic rationale underlying this view.

RANDOM WALK. Nelson and Plosser (1982) argue that real per capita output and many other economic time series behave as if they have random walk components (much like the log of stock prices). They also argue that Solow's technology series also behaves like a random walk. The observation that the log of productivity follows a random walk with drift (drift meaning the changes have a nonzero mean) has the following important implications:

First, a random walk is a nonstationary stochastic process, which means that it possesses no affinity for any particular mean. Random walks are also referred to as stochastic trend because while they may exhibit growth, they do not fluctuate about any particular deterministic path.

Second, the fact that productivity grows over time, raises some additional complications for the neoclassical model described previously. If, for example, output and consumption grew at different rates, in the long run, the consumption/output ratio would be driven to zero or one. To prevent this, it is usually required that these per capita values converge to constants, but equal growth rates, so that the model possesses steady-state growth. Of particular importance is the requirement that permanent technological progress must be expressible as labor augmenting or Harrod-neutral.

Third, King, Plosser, and Rebelo (1988) and King, Plosser, Stock, and Watson (1987) show that the neoclassical model with random walk technological progress implies that output, consumption, and investment per capita will all contain a common random walk component or stochastic trend. This structure is consistent with the empirical observations of Nelson and Plosser discussed above. But hours worked per capita will not contain a stochastic growth component.

INTEGRATED APPROACH. The permanent change in productivity sets in motion a series of dynamic responses that move Robinson Crusoe and an economy toward a new growth path. For example, 1 percent permanent (once and for all) change in labor productivity in the long run leads to a 1 percent permanent increase in the level of capital stock, consumption, output, and investment once the transitory dynamics have been dissipated. These transitory dynamics are important for understanding fluctuations. The responses and thus the fluctuations that are present in the model are the result of the same factors that generate economic growth—namely, technical change in addition to the capital per capita worker. The RBC model, therefore, provides an integrated approach to the theory of growth and fluctuations.

RBC and the 1954 to 1985 U.S. Economy

The simple neoclassical model described earlier is clearly an incomplete model of the U.S. economy. Nevertheless, useful insights into the properties of the model can be obtained by providing a more quantitative assessment of the model's explanatory power. They take the Cobb-Douglas formulation, logarithmic preferences, and the random walk properties of the technology shifts. Based on these, approximate optimal decisions of Robinson Crusoe can be obtained and used to calculate how he will respond to the Solow technology shifts.

SUMMARY STATISTICS FOR THE U.S. ECONOMY. All the series (investment, consumption, hours worked, and wages) are highly correlated with output and thus are procyclical. The lowest correlation with output is exhibited by real wage growth (Plosser, 1989, p. 62, table 1).

PRODUCTIVITY SHIFTS. Plosser considers as a first approximation it seems acceptable to view the level of productivity as a random-walk phenomenon (1989, p. 63, fig. 1).

REAL BUSINESS CYCLE. Given the form of preferences and technology, the model is used to obtain the responses to the simple neoclassical model to observed productivity shifts (Plosser, 1989, table 1). The model produces sample means that are very close to the data for output, consumption, and hours but are too low for ivestment and too high for wages. There are correlation coefficients of the predicted outcomes with the actual series and range from 0.52 for hours worked to 0.87 for output (table 1, panel B).

Then Plosser (1989, p. 65) says that "To many economists, the whole idea that such a simple model with no government, no money, no market failures of any kind, rational expectations, no adjustment costs and identical agents could replicate actual experience this well, is very surprising." He considers RBC models to have strong explanatory power. The results also verify technology shifts subject to a random walk because they are obtained by feeding the measured technological shocks.

Conclusions

The basic framework of RBC analysis is the neoclassical model of capital accumulation. This is the natural starting point to begin the study of dynamic fluctuations. While frequently interpreted as a model of economic growth, the neoclassical model generates fluctuations in response to external disturbances that resemble business cycles. RBC models do not have to be confined to analyzing only technological or productivity shocks. Nevertheless, these real technological disturbances generate rich and neglected dynamics in the basic neoclassical model that appear to count for a substantial portion of observed fluctuations.

RBC theory is still in its infancy and thus remains an incomplete theory of the business cycle.[4] Yet RBC progress to date has had a significant impact on research in economics. In particular, simple RBC models have demonstrated that equilibrium models are not necessarily inconsistent with many characteristics attributed to the business cycle.

Some Comments

RBC models deal with "the idealized state of dynamic equilibrium" argued by Hicks (1939), who stated that these models must be at the core of any understanding economists will provide of business cycles. This type of model "gives us a way of assessing the extent or degree of disequilibrium," and it also gives us some norms for policy targets. In these respects, this approach might be useful. However, some problems and difficulties arise that may cause us to discard the usefulness of the models.

This section addresses some difficulties and weaknesses of RBC models:[5] that the difficulty with continuity is shared by the classical dichotomy and the RBC theory; that Solow's residual may not be proper evidence regarding exogenous technological disturbances, suggesting an endogenous explanation regarding productivity change; that the weakness of the equilibrium model can be explored from various viewpoints, especially when explaining the actual economy; and that the RBC models can be related to this book's research.

The Classical Dichotomy

According to the classical theories, real variables are determined by the Walrasian system, and nominal variables are determined by the equilibrium in the money market. Then the money market can be ignored. This is called the classical dichotomy (Patinkin, 1956).

Mankiw (1989, p. 80) argues that the RBC theory embraces the classical dichotomy. Nominal variables are assumed to have no role in explaining fluctuations in real variables. Under the classical dichotomy, it is assumed that nominal variables such as wages and prices adjust instantly to clear the market. However, many nominal wages are fixed by long-term labor contracts, and many product prices remain unchanged for long periods of time. Once the inflexibility of wages and prices is admitted into a macroeconomic model, the classical dichotomy and the irrelevance of money quickly disappear.[6]

RBC theorists assume that fluctuations in employment are fully voluntary. Under the recession the unemployment rate rises, but it is not plausible to say that the workers are on the supply curve and the labor markets are cleared. As Mankiw (1989, p. 86) says, "over the typical business cycle, employment varies substantially while the determinants of labor supply—the real wage and the real interest rate—vary only slightly." It is accordingly unlikely that individuals would be so responsive to intertemporal relative prices.

Technological Disturbances (Solow's Residual)

According to the RBC model, business cycles are caused by the forces that change Walrasian equilibrium. Many sorts of macroeconomic disturbances generate fluctuations, among which technological disturbances make the central role. They assume fluctuations in the rate of technological change followed Solow argument or thesis. Then they calculate the annual percentage rate of change in technology that follows Solow, considering "it seems to be acceptable (as a first approximation) to view the level of productivity as a random walk" (Plosser, p. 63).

Could Solow's residual[7] calculated by the Cobb-Douglas function (assuming a constant returns to scale) be evidence for exogenous technological disturbances? Mankiw himself calculates the Solow residual and the percentage change in output yearly since 1948, arguing that one might say the aggregate production function varies substantially from year to year. There are big year-to-year changes in total productivity growth; for example, it fell by 3.5 percent in 1982 and rose by 3.4 percent in 1984 (Mankiw, 1989, p. 84).

It may be possible to explain the change of productivity growth by the endogenous factors rather than exogenous factors. The writer considers that it will be explained by the combined effect of the change of capacity utilization and labor hoarding,[8] etc. It is basically explained without technology progress. In a recession, the capacity utilization of capital decreases, labor hoarding occurs, and then the ratio of overhead to direct labors increases. All these factors in general decrease the productivity growth. In a boom, productivity rises because the capacity utilization of capital grows, the hoarded laborers begin to put out greater effort, and output increases without a large increase in measured labor input.

Technology progress aggravates these changes. Taking technology progress into consideration, keeping a constant returns to scale is very hard to do.[9] The situation is rather an increasing returns to scale.

Equilibrium Model

The RBC model, in spirit and structure, is an extension of the usual competitive general equilibrium model and shares its basic properties.

Akerlof, Rose, and Yellen (1988, pp. 67–68) argue that equilibrium models of the business cycle have already failed many tests. First, job leavers rise and vacancies decline as the unemployment rate falls. On average, people appear to value their jobs more highly in bad times than in good. Second, the demand shocks of World War II, the Vietnam War, and Mrs. Thatcher's successful policy of disinflation, as well as Mr. Volcker's similar policy, all produced changes in equilibrium output, long after the policies were announced (and seen to be credible).

As Plosser (1989) admits, the fact that productivity grows over time series raises some additional complications for the basic neoclassical model. The model requires per capita values (capital stock, consumption, output, and investment) to converge to constants but growth rates to be equal, so that the model possesses steady-state growth. Once the transitory dynamics have been dissipated, an economy moves on a new steady growth path. In this respect, of particular importance is the requirement that permanent technological progress must be expressible as labor augmenting or Harrod-neutral.

The equilibrium growth model needs a broad set of conditions to have steady-state growth. These conditions are (1) various per capita values converging to constants, but equal growth rates in the long run, and (2) labor augmenting or Harrod neutral technological progress. The question remains. Are these assumptions plausible or stylized facts?

First, steady-state growth is the idealized state of dynamic equilibrium, which is attained on the neoclassical assumptions when the broad set of conditions are fulfilled. It is a question of logic rather than facts. Logical consistency is very important, but an actual growth path will not be explained only by that.

Second, dealing with an economy in the long run, using the Cobb-Douglas production function, causes some difficulties to arise. First, the relative share of labor fluctuates and is not always fluctuating around the same level: it sometimes shows a large (one-decade or so) increasing trend or decreasing trend.[10] Second, the actual economy seems to be under increasing returns to scale rather than a constant returns to scale. Referring to the growth rates of productivity in Chapter 2 (Figures 2.8a, 2.9a, and 2.10a), actual productivity growth is not likely to occur on the production function in the long run. The growth rate fluctuations will be explained by the endogenous factors (see the comment on technological disturbances).

Third, we seldom see a steady growth path. Various per capita values have difficulty in remaining constants (at equal growth rates) in an actual economy. Among these, for example, investment values suffer from the largest fluctuations. The fourth is the problem of the Harrod-neutral technical progress. When the business cycle and economic growth are observed in terms of several years or a couple of decades time period, it is arguable whether the Harrod-neutral technical progress is a stylized fact. The argument in Chapter 3 was rather negative.[11]

What Do the RBC Models Explain?

Despite the fact that the RBC model is extremely simple, it can replicate actual experience surprisingly well. Plosser uses summary statistics for the United States (Plosser, 1989, p. 62, table 1), in which all the series (investment, consumption, hours worked, and wages) are highly correlated with output and thus are procyclical. Feeding the measured technological shocks (which are procyclical) to the model produced sample means that were very close to the data for output, consumption, and hours but were too low for investment and too high for wages. Among others, the poorest fit was the growth rate of hours worked.

However, the RBC approach has weaknesses as follows. First, the measured technological shocks, which are assumed to follow a random walk, are fed into the real business cycle model. The results heavily depend on these input. As was mentioned earlier, these measured technological shocks should be explained endogenously. Second, the poor results showing that the sample means for investment is too low and for wages too high, and the poorest fit is for hours worked, perhaps depend on their treatment of employment.[12] Hours worked per capita will not contain a stochastic growth. However, the volume of employment actually changes in the business cycle, particularly the rate of unemployment,

The RBC model has procyclical real wage growth rate, although prediction is poor, with the correlation coefficient 0.52 of the predicted outcomes with the actual series for the United States. However, so far as the models depend on the Cobb-Douglas production function and on an assumption of labor augmenting or Harrod-neutral technological progress, their predictions of the profit rate and the profit share are difficult. In our actual economy these variables are subject to changes in the business cycle. (refer to the facts established in Chapter 2).[13]

THE NEW KEYNESIAN THEORY

Introduction

Ball, Mankiw, and Romer (1988; hereafter BMR) describe Keynesian economics as follows. According to the Keynesian view, fluctuations in output arise largely from fluctuations in nominal aggregate demand, which are rigid. But in Keynesian models of the 1970s, the crucial nominal rigidities were assumed rather than explained—assumed directly, as in disequilibrium models, or introduced through theoretically arbitrary assumptions about labor contracts.[14] This does not go with microeconomic teaching. Thus the 1970s and early 1980s saw many economists turn away from Keynesian theories and toward new classical models with flexible wages and prices (pp. 1–2).

The Keynesian theory lacked a microeconomic foundation. However, in the middle 1980s Keynesian economics made much progress in providing a microeconomic explanation of why nominal rigidity should exist and how sluggish nominal adjustment might involve minor costs for a single firm but major costs for the economy as a whole.

The forty-fifth conference of the Brookings Panel on Economic Activity was held in Washington, DC, on April 7, 1988. BMR presented a paper entitled "The New Keynesian Economics and the Output-Inflation Tradeoff." The paper, a summary, comments on it, and discussion, as well as other presented papers, were published in the *Brookings Papers* (1988). The following sections present my explanation of the theory that follows this BMR paper.

The Theory

The BMR paper is comprehensive. It consists of a summary of recent research[15] followed by the construction of a new Keynesian model by incorporating some of the central ideas of their research.[16] The model is tested using international data.

The Model

BMR explain their general characteristics in the model as follows. Their model of price adjustment is similar in spirit to those of Taylor (1979, 1980) and Blanchard (1983, 1986). The model is set in continuous time. The economy contains imperfectly competitive firms that change prices at discrete intervals rather than continuously because adjustments are costly. Price setting is staggered, with an equal proportion of firms changing prices at every instant. The crucial departure from Taylor and Blanchard is that the length of time between price changes, and hence the rate at which the price level adjusts to shocks, is endogenous (p. 20).

The model is constructed under imperfect competition. They assume that:

(i) A representative firm i's profits depend on three variables—y = aggregate spending, $p_i - p$ = firm i's relative price, and θ_i = a firm-specific shock (all variables are in logs). The aggregate price level p is defined as the average of prices across firms.
(ii) The elasticity of firm i's profit-maximizing real price, $p_i^* - p$, with respect to y is a positive constant v.
(iii) The elasticity of $p_i^* - p$ with respect to θ_i is one and that θ_i has zero mean.

Thus they write the profit-maximizing real price as

$$p_i^*(t) - p(t) = v[y(t) - \bar{y}(t)] + \theta_i(t), \; v > 0, \qquad (5)$$

where $\bar{y}$ is the natural rate of output—the level at which, if θ_i equals its mean, the firm desires a relative price of one.[17]

Then they assume that

(iv) An adjustment cost leads firms to change prices only at intervals of length λ, which for simplicity is constant over time. Each price change has a fixed cost F, so adjustment costs per period are F/λ.

Maximizing profits is equivalent to minimizing profit losses from two sources: adjustment costs and deviations of price from the profit-maximizing level. They approximate the latter by

$$(1/2)K(p_i - p_i^*)^2,$$

where K is the negative of the second derivative of profits with respect to $p_i^* - p_i$. Thus firm i's loss per unit of time is

$$\frac{F}{\lambda} + \frac{1}{\lambda} \cdot \frac{1}{2} K \int_{s=0}^{\lambda} E_i [p_i^*(t+s) - p_i]^2 ds. \tag{6}$$

Minimization of equation (6) implies a simple rule for choosing p_i:

$$p_i = \frac{1}{\lambda} \int_{s=0}^{\lambda} E_i p_i^*(t+s) ds. \tag{7}$$

That is, a firm sets its price to the average of its expected profit-maximizing prices for the period when the price is in effect.

Assuming the log of nominal aggregate demand x,

$$x \equiv y + p,$$

is exogenous and follows the continuous-time analogue of a random walk with drift, then they have

$$x(t) = gt + \sigma_x W(t), \tag{8}$$

where

$W(t)$ = Wiener process,
gt = trend growth of g per unit of time, and
$\sigma_x W(t)$ = random walk innovations with variance σ_x^2 per unit of time (σ_x = standard deviation of demand).

Furthermore, they assume that

(vi) The natural rate of output grows smoothly at rate μ:

$$\bar{y}(t) = \mu t. \tag{9}$$

Along with the process for $x(t)$, this implies that average inflation is $g - \mu$.

Finally, they assume that

(vii) The firm-specific disturbances, the θ_i's, are uncorrelated across firms and follow continuous-time random walks whose innovations have mean zero and variance σ_θ^2 per unit of time. (σ_θ = standard deviation of firm-specific shocks, and σ_θ^2 = variance of firm-specific shocks.)

A Frequency of Price Changes

The solution for the behavior of the price level takes the form

$$p(t) = (g - \mu)t + \int_{s=0}^{\infty} w(s; \lambda) dZ(t-s), \tag{10}$$

where $dZ(t-s) \equiv \sigma_x dW(t-s)$ is the innovation in aggregate demand at $t-s$ (the first term = average inflation; the second term = the effects of shocks). The term $w(s; \lambda)$ gives the effect of a demand shock at $t-s$ on the price level at t. Assuming $\nu < 1$, $w(s; \lambda)$ equals zero when $s = 0$, increases with s, and approaches 1 as s approaches infinity. The crucial result about $w(\cdot)$ concerns the frequency of price changes; when $\nu < 1$, $w(s; \lambda)$ is decreasing in λ.

The behavior of real output follows directly from the behavior of the price level, the stochastic process for aggregate demand, and the identity $y = x - p$:

$$y(t) - \bar{y}(t) = \int_{s=0}^{\infty} [1 - w(s; \lambda)] dZ(t-s). \tag{11}$$

The sizes of the real effects of nominal shocks are given by $1 - w(\cdot)$.

Finally, equation (11) implies an expression for the variance of output:

$$E\{[y(t) - \bar{y}(t)]^2\} = \sigma_x^2 \int_{s=0}^{\infty} [1 - w(s; \lambda)]^2 ds. \tag{12}$$

The variance of output depends on the variance of demand shocks σ_x^2 and the size of the effects of shocks $1 - w(\cdot)$.

Then they derive an equilibrium condition defining the equilibrium interval between price changes. The value of a firm's loss function, L(equation 6), is affected by both λ_i (firm i) and λ. Minimization of $L(\lambda_i, \lambda)$ with respect to λ_i yields the first-order condition $\partial L(\lambda_i, \lambda)/\partial \lambda_i = 0$. A symmetric Nash equilibrium for λ, λ^E is defined implicitly by setting $\lambda_i = \lambda$ in this condition:

$$\left. \frac{\partial L(\lambda_i, \lambda^E)}{\partial \lambda_i} \right|_{\lambda_i = \lambda^E} = 0. \tag{13}$$

An interval λ is an equilibrium if, when λ is chosen throughout the economy, it is in firm i's interest to choose λ as well. They find that λ is decreasing in $\bar{\pi}$, σ_x, and σ_θ, where $\bar{\pi} \equiv g - \mu$ is the average inflation rate.

These results, along with the results about the effects of λ, imply that the Phillips curve is steeper when $\bar{\pi}$, σ_x, or σ_θ is larger. Higher average inflation reduces the interval between price changes, which in turn raises $w(\cdot)$, the proportion of a shock that is passed into prices. A larger variance of aggregate or firm-specific shocks also reduces λ and thus raises $w(\cdot)$. These results imply that increases in $\bar{\pi}$, σ_x, or σ_θ lead to decreases in $1 - w(\cdot)$, the real effect of shocks.

Conclusions

BMR examine the short-run tradeoff between output and inflation using international data. As a result, they assert, it is a robust finding that "this trade-off is affected by the average rate of inflation" (p. 59).

Then they conclude with three important implications of the finding (pp. 59–60). First, it provides evidence against new classical theories of the output-inflation tradeoff. Lucas's theory predicts that the tradeoff should not be related to average inflation. It is therefore inconsistent with their empirical results.[18]

Second, their finding supports new Keynesian theories of the business cycle that derive nominal rigidities from optimizing behavior. Their theoretical model of price adjustment shows that macroeconomic effects of the sort they observe can result from empirically plausible microeconomic parameters.

Third, their finding implies that the tradeoff faced by macroeconomic policy makers depends on the average rate of inflation and that the tradeoff changes when the average rate of inflation changes.

Some Comments

The traditional Keynesian theory lacked a microeconomic foundation. BMR consider this as the main reason why many economists in the 1970s and early 1980s turned away from Keynesian theories and toward new classical models with flexible wages and prices. They tried to provide microeconomic foundations for nominal rigidities by introducing optimal behavior. They incorporated two innovations (the introduction of imperfect competition and product market rigidities), which were the central ideas of recent research, into a new Keynesian model of price adjustment.

The question remains: is their new Keynesian model successful? Some questions remain unanswered. First, a difficulty exists in general in reconciling macroeconomics with microeconomic explanations based on profit-maximization principles. Second, is their assumption of price changes plausible? Third, the new Keynesian model seems to have difficulty explaining the established fact of productivity change. Fourth, comments on the theory presented by Christopher A. Sims (1988) need to be addressed. Fifth, Dore (1993) criticizes new Keynesian theory presented in his latest book. Finally, the new Keynesian theory can be explained in relation to the purpose of the research presented in this book.

Increasing Returns to Scale

It seems to be possible to observe a trend increase in productivity in a macroeconomy,[19] although the trend sometimes shifts. The rate of average productivity growth based on GDP in percentages, during the years 1970 to 1992, was 2.04 (the United Kingdom), 0.70 (the United States), and 3.15 (Japan). The trend is observed by Figures 2.10a for Japan, 2.8a for the United Kingdom and to lesser extent 2.9a for the United States in Chapter 2. The trend is due to technological progress in a broad sense, which causes *increasing returns to scale.*[20]

When increasing returns to scale are considered on a macro level, it is fairly difficult to find a microeconomic foundation that is compatible with it.

Microeconomic explanations are primarily based on profit-maximization principles, which generally assume constant returns to scale.

Suppose that this treatment based on profit maximization is in the first approximation. What comes the next? It is not easy to deal with the analysis under increasing returns to scale. Even if it is possible, what basic results in the first approach are applicable in the next plausible stage? It is a fairly hopeless task to reconcile these, because the basic features between these two (constant returns to scale and increasing returns to scale) differ in principle. According to Kaldor's strong criticism, the principles based on the first approach would be totally corrupted in the second plausible approach.[21] Thus the first approach based on the profit maximization is of little value.

Price Changes

Relating to price changes, BMR (1988, p. 20) assume that imperfectly competitive firms "change prices at discrete intervals rather than continuously; price setting is staggered, with an equal proportion of firms changing prices at every instant; an adjustment cost leads firms to change prices only at intervals of length λ, which for simplicity is constant over time."

However, while "staggered price setting" is acceptable, it is not always plausible to consider an equal proportion of firms changing prices at every instant. The groups of firms that change prices during expansion years in the economy are rather easy to detect. By contrast the groups of firms that change prices during contraction years are less obvious. It becomes difficult when "a firm sets its price to the average of its expected profit-maximizing prices for the period when the price is [in fact] in effect" (p. 22). This is expressed by equation (7):

$$p_i = \frac{1}{\lambda} \int_{s=0}^{\lambda} E_t p_i^*(t + s) ds.$$

If the size of a price change in recession is not moderate (rather larger) reflecting BMR's expected price change rule, then groups of the firms under imperfect competition face rapid loss of demand while other groups of firms who do not change prices will not. In this case it is not plausible to consider an equal proportion of firms changing prices. Some firms may postpone price changes, and some others would reduce the price increases below the average of its expected profit-maximizing prices for the period when the price is in effect.

Therefore the price increase (price level) is not always smooth. It sometimes has accelerated periods or decelerated periods, as can be observed from time to time. Their price-setting assumption based on optimizing behavior does not seem to be plausible. Robert Hall (BMR, 1988, pp. 79–80) argues that most prices are much more flexible. He is skeptical about the U.S. economy being characterized as a collection of firms that set prices and meet demand at the price.

Figure 5.1. Windfall Profits and Losses in Imperfect Competition

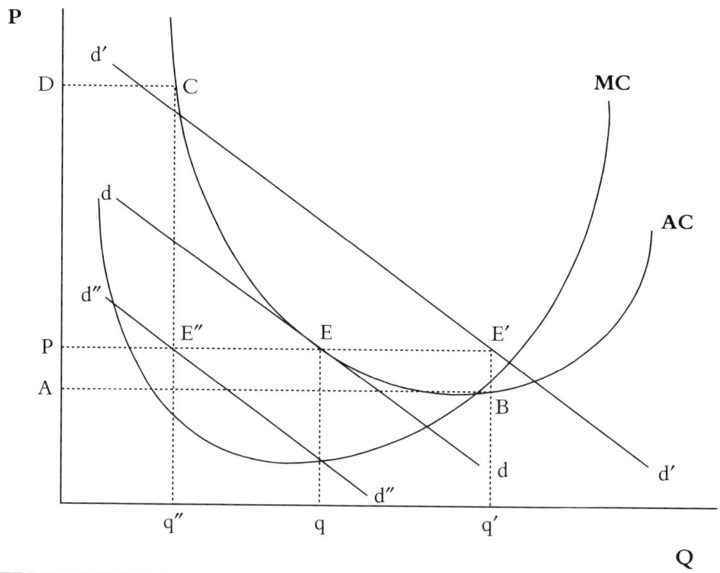

Productivity Change in the Business Cycle

In the new Keynesian model, BMR assume a representative firm in imperfect competition. It is likely to be considered monopolistic competition presented by Chamberlain (1933). Suppose that the representative firm is facing a downward slope in the demand curve as depicted in Figure 5.1.

Horizontal and vertical axes reflect output and price, respectively. *dd* is a demand curve for the representative firm. In the monopolistic competitive equilibrium, the price is p at equilibrium point E. The curve *dd* is a gradient of AC at E. There is no windfall profits and losses at E. When the total demand increases, the demand for the representative firm shifts upward to $d'd'$. If the firm does not change the price at p, and an AC (average cost) of the firm is A at production level q', then the volume of excess profits becomes $ABE'p$. In contrast, when the total demand decreases, the demand curve for the firm shifts downward to $d''d''$. However, when the price is maintained at p level, then the firm suffers a loss of $pE''CD$ because the AC is C at production level q''.

Suppose that production level q' and q'' are peaks and troughs, respectively. First, start from the trough at production level q''. The production increases in accordance with an increase of demand. As the slope of AC curve becomes gentler, the growth rate in labor productivity (Q/L) becomes smaller. This occurs with typical observations of productivity change. In the first expansion year after trough, labor productivity grows sharply, and then the growth rate is gradually decelerated. We here consider the productivity change by deducting trend growth (simply an average of growth rate during the observation period) from actual figures.

Second, when the representative firm starts from the peak, the reverse process goes on if the change in productivity happens along the production curve. However, our fact finding in Chapter 2 opposes this prediction. Labor productivity shows a sharp decrease in the first year of contraction. If it happens on the production curve in Figure 5.1, the decrease in productivity will be accelerated as the demand decreases. A typical fact is that the productivity growth in the first year of contraction becomes negative, and then it gradually shows positive growth. This means that the firm is not on the production curve, which might otherwise be expected during business recession.

Sims's Comments

Sims (1988) shows some disagreements with BMR (1988) in his comments.

First of all, the BMR paper asserts that Keynesian economics fell into disrepute because it could not provide a justification based on "optimizing behaviour for its assumption of price rigidity." However, Sims argues that one of the accomplishments of Keynesian economics (and a main reason for its original appeal) is that it proceeded boldly to legitimize "money illusion" and "nonclearing markets" as primitive assumptions in economic models. It was and still is a strength of Keynesian economics that it does not make a fetish of modeling based on optimizing behavior (p. 75).

Therefore, Keynesian economics declined because it failed to offer a true explanation about how nominal rigidities respond to the economic environment, not because it failed to offer an explanation based on optimizing behavior. Sims (1988, p. 76) says that "It may not be the time yet for a new wave in macroeconomic theory, but if it is, I expect that it will come from rediscovering the Keynesian willingness to confront irrationality and market failure."

Then, relating to their empirical analysis, Sims also criticizes that the data presented by the authors in fact provide no support at all for their claim that the level of inflation affects the degree of price rigidity. He explains his reasoning as follows (1988, p. 77)

> In the authors' sample, the standard deviation and the level of inflation have a correlation of 0.92. The question is then whether they have found anything more than the tendency—expected from neoclassical equilibrium theories—for economies with highly variable inflation to have a lower regression coefficient for output on aggregate demand. The authors put aside any direct test of this proposition by pointing to the identity, equation 16, in the paper.

The writer supports these views, among others, those relating to disagreements with the BMR's assumptions based on optimizing behaviour.[22]

Dore's Comment

The new Keynesian theory adopts the representative agent as an analytical starting point, which is specifically a neoclassical invention in economics. Dore (1993, sec. 7.3) criticizes this representative agent framework, saying that "the proposition that characteristics of the aggregate merely reflect characteristics of individual units may in fact be a fallacy of composition" (p. 125).[23]

Dore argues that the existence of price rigidity due to menu cost at the level of the firm is quite consistent with complete aggregate price flexibility, as demonstrated by Caplin and Spulber (1987). Furthermore, he takes up the study of Caballero (1991) that analyzes the sources of several fallacies of composition in representative agent models, presenting (Dore, 1993, p. 127) Caballero's clear conclusions that

> Asymmetric pricing policies at the firm level do not necessarily imply asymmetries at the aggregate level; and asymmetries at the aggregate price level need not come from asymmetries at the firm level. Similarly, asymmetric factor adjustment costs at the firm level need not imply asymmetric responses of the capital stock and the level of employment to positive and negative shocks. *To assert otherwise is to commit the fallacy of composition.*"

Dore (1993, p. 128) agrees with these conclusions, concluding himself that "the representative agent framework is the most serious limitation of New Keynesian business cycle theory, despite some of its other merits. It rests on a fallacy of composition. Such micro-based models do not yield a satisfactory theory of business cycles."[24]

The new classicals in which RBC models are included are not exempted from this critique relating to the representative agent framework. For the representative agent is specifically a neoclassical invention in economics, and the use of this as the basis of analysis is the new classical method.

What the New Keynesian Theory Explains

The new Keynesians attempt to obtain Keynesian results (such as an underemployment equilibrium) from microeconomics and representative models.

Dore (1993, p. 215) assesses this theory, concluding that "New Keynesians are less concerned about explaining the stylized facts; to them the 'business cycle' is the underemployment equilibrium, the recession, and not just the associated welfare losses; each recession leaves the economy's capital stock lower than it would have been."

The purpose of the BMR paper is to provide evidence supporting new Keynesian theories. They are much concerned with pointing out a simple prediction of Keynesian models that contradicts other leading macroeconomic theories and with demonstrating that it holds in actual economies. Therefore, the BMR paper does not address the business cycle.

However, a couple of things would be predicted by the model, from the viewpoint of this research, to explain the changes of macroeconomic variables in the business cycle.

First, procyclical changes of wages are explained assuming efficiency wages. Brainard and Perry (1988, p. xxvii) remark on this in their summary of the study of Greenwald and Stiglitz (1988)[25] that

> According to efficiency wage theory, higher real wages improve labor productivity by eliciting greater effort from workers attracting a high-quality labor supply, and reducing turnover. . . . Firms believe that increases in demand are associated with a reduction of risk to the marginal product of labor, the risk-adjusted marginal product may actually rise, rather than decline, during an expansion, warranting a rise in the real wage, in accordance with the facts.

Second, what do they explain about the change of the labor share or the profit share? The growth-rate formula of the relative share of labor ρ_l, which was obtained from the identity ($\rho_l = W/Y$), was

$$\hat{\rho}_l = \hat{\omega}_m - (\hat{e} + \hat{\mu}).^{26} \tag{2}$$

Replacing ($\hat{\omega}_m - \hat{e}$) with the real wage growth rate $\hat{\omega}$ results in

$$\hat{\rho}_l = \hat{\omega} - \hat{\mu}. \tag{2a}$$

By equation (2a), even if real wages are procyclycal, they can not predict the relative share of labor without setting some clear relationship between productivity and the business cycle. In this respect, a Cobb-Douglas production function in the traditional Keynesian model will not be a solution. A procyclical change in productivity is a well-known fact, so the new Keynesian theory needs to deal with productivity change to explain this. Therefore, we consider that they have difficulty in predicting the change of labor share and the profit share.

Third, the profit rate seems to move procyclically on a micro level. As was discussed previously in this chapter in "Productivity Change in the Business Cycle," profits of the representative firm will increase when it faces increasing demand, and vice versa when it faces decreasing demand. Then the profit rate is likely to move procyclically. (Consider the change of operating rate of capital in the business cycle).

As Dore mentioned, the new Keynesian theories are less concerned about explaining the stylized facts. Their model has the possibility of explaining the procyclical change of real wages and the profit rate but has difficulty in explaining the changes of the labor share and productivity in the economy. One of their weakest points is their treatment of productivity in explaining the distribution of income in the business cycle.

CONCLUSIONS: SOME REMARKS ON EACH THEORY

The two theories that explain the business cycle—neoclassical theory and Keynesian theory—have been discussed in terms of their reinterpretation as new models. These two theories have more or less opposed each other. Until recently the fundamental criticism of the neoclassicals toward Keynesian theory was the lack of microeconomic foundations (Friedman, 1968; Lucas, 1976; and Plosser, 1989). The neoclassical theory has a strong foundation in microeconomics based on profit-maximization principles. They emphasize the equilibrium model.

Keynesians admit that their theory has a weakness in explaining the actual economy, especially in the 1970s and early 1980s. One of the powerful ways to cope with this weakness is to provide sound microeconomic foundations based on optimal behavior. The other way, as Sims argues, is to seek a true explanation without taking an optimal behavior assumption (BMR is a powerful example of the former).[27]

Both RBC and BMR models were applied to an actual economy. Plosser applied the RBC model to the 1954 to 1985 U.S. economy. Then he concluded the results were satisfactory, saying that the whole idea that the model "could replicate actual experience this well is very surprising" (Plosser, 1989, p. 65). BMR tested their theoretical results by estimating the output-inflation tradeoff for forty-three industrialized countries and examining the relationship between the tradeoff and average inflation and demand variability. They concluded that their main results were satisfactory and robust as well.

Mankiw (1989, p. 88) points out some criteria for assessing a model: "A good theory has two characteristics: internal consistency and external consistency. An internally consistent theory is one that is parsimonious; it invokes no ad hoc or peculiar axioms. An externally consistent theory is one that fits the facts; it makes empirically refutable predictions that are not refuted." He continues (p. 89): "The choice between alternative theories of the business cycle—in particular, between real business cycle theory and new Keynesian theory—is partly a choice between internal and external consistency."

Both theory have their weaknesses. The RBC theory strongly seeks internal consistency rather than external consistency. As a result the model becomes an equilibrium model. To apply the model to the dynamic movement in the economy, they introduce a stochastic process (a random walk). The fluctuations are caused by exogenous disturbances such as technological disturbances, but it should be explained endogenously. Looking at the facts, it becomes apparent that (1) keeping the classical dichotomy becomes difficult,

(2) unemployment may not be fully voluntary, particularly in a recession, (3) the aggregate production function may vary substantially from year-to-year; and (4) broad set of their equilibrium conditions is not always plausible.

The new Keynesian theory seeks external consistency and internal consistency as well by providing microeconomic foundations. The two innovations greatly attributed to the development of the model. However, treatment of price setting based on optimizing behavior does not seem to be plausible. The model has difficulty in explaining the change in productivity in the business cycle.

The RBC theory has difficulty in explaining particularly the change of variables in the labor market. This model explains procyclical real wages by simulations, though their prediction is poor. However, productivity change is not explained but given exogenously. Their predictions of the changes of the profit rate and the relative share are difficult. The new Keynesian theory also has difficulty in explaining the change of the variables in the labor market. Their model possibly can explain the procyclical change of real wages and the profit rate but has difficulty in explaining the changes of the labor share and productivity.

Both schools strive for internal consistency and external consistency in their theories. Despite the fact that each model has some unrealistic assumptions and also has some difficulties in explaining actual changes of variables, each believes that its predicted results are valid—that the results from the BMR model are surprisingly good and that those from the new Keynesian model are robust. It can be argued that more consistent theoretical explanations reflecting on the facts are needed if each model is to persist in its claims of interpretative value. In this respect, a recent growing body of studies relating to fallacies of composition deserves attention: these studies demonstrate that the representative agent framework that is taken by both the RBC models and the new Keynesian theory leads to a fallacy of composition.

NOTES

1. Plosser presents two economists (Friedman, 1968, and Lucas, 1976) who forcefully demonstrated examples of this flaw in critical aspects of the Keynesian reasoning and set the stage for modern macroeconomics.

2. A more analytical summary of a model of RBC is presented in Plosser's appendix (1989, pp. 72–75). Here the summary of RBC follows Plosser in a descriptive rather than specified way.

3. Under most specifications of preferences and production functions, it is impossible to solve analytically this maximization problem for the optimal decision rules of Robinson Crusoe. Then it is necessary to compute approximate solutions to Robinson Crusoe's choice problem in the neighborhood of the steady state.

4. Plosser presents the following research agenda with some arguments: multisector extensions, labor markets, endogenous growth, money, and strategies for estimation and hypothesis testing (1989, pp. 67–71).

5. See "Dore's Comment" later in this chapter for the methodology argument. The criticism that the representative agent framework leads to a *fallacy of composition* holds true of the RBC models. Refer to Matthews (1994) for Dore's book review.

6. Mankiw points out that much of the early work in the neoclassical revolution of the 1970s attempted to destroy the classical dichotomy without abandoning the fundamental axiom of continuous market clearing (Lucas, 1972, 1973). These models were based on the assumption that individuals have imperfect information regarding prices (Mankiw, 1989, p. 80). Plosser (1989) admits that "the role of money in equilibrium theory of growth and fluctuations is not well understood and thus remains an open issue" (p. 70).

7. Robert Solow (1957) suggested a simple way of measuring technological change. Consider any constant returns to scale production with neutral technological change such as that given by

$$Y_t = \theta_t F\,(K_t,\ N_t),$$

Where Y_t is output at time t, K is the capital input, N is the labor input, and θ measures productivity shifts over time. He constructed estimates of U.S. technological change using data from 1909 to 1949. Then, he argued on his estimates and concluded that about 85 percent of the real per capita growth during this period was accounted for by technological change or productivity and only about 15 percent by increases in capital per worker. Solow's view of technological change included anything that shifted the production function other than measurable capital and labor.

8. Mankiw presents Labor hoarding and other "off the production function" behavior as a standard explanation (1989, p. 84).

9. Plosser (1989) makes a remark on technology as an RBC research agenda item. Relying so heavily on such exogenous unobservable progress is unsatisfactory. Work by Uzawa (1965), Romer (1986), and Lucas (1988) suggests that the key to obtaining growth as an endogenous outcome of technology is to eliminate the diminishing returns in the production process. King and Rebelo (1986, 1988) provide examples of this strategy whose idea is to permit human capital (labor-augmenting technical change) to be produced using physical capital and human capital as inputs to a constant returns technology.

10. Refer to Figure 2.2a for the United Kingdom, Figure 2.3a for the United States, and to some extent Figure 2.4a for Japan in Chapter 2. Longer period references (1950 to 1982) for the United Kingdom and (1950 to 1985) for Japan are available from Iyoda (1985, fig. 1) and Iyoda (1987, fig. 1), respectively.

11. Refer to "Arguments on the Historical Constancies" in Chapter 3.

12. See Dore (1993, pp. 90–91) for an argument on the treatment of employment in the RBC model.

13. A comprehensive discussion on the RBC theory is beyond the scope of this book. For this for example, refer to Dore's (1993) discussion, particularly his section 6.4. After discussions, Dore concludes that (p. 93)

> RBC is indeed an equilibrium account, provided output can be decomposed into a permanent and a cyclical component. The cyclical component is then expressed as a sum of exogenous random shocks, which can be done only by arbitrarily imposing a particular lag structure on the exogenous technology shock parameter. . . . The model is presented as a cyclical model by simulations and calibrations which generate a series that looks like a GNP time series, although fluctuations in employment are largely ignored.

However, the integral relationship between output, employment, and inflation, which, Dore considers, is important, cannot be explained by the RBC model: "Thus it fails to reflect the stylized facts of chapter 2" (p. 93).

14. They refer to Barro and Grossman (1971) and Malinvaud (1977) for disequilibrium models and to Fischer (1977) and Gray (1978) for contract models.

15. BMR refer to a substantial body of research literature, the most recent and useful of which are listed here.

For small nominal frictions and large nominal rigidities, see Mankiw (1985), Akerlof and Yellen (1985), Blanchard and Kiyotaki (1987), and Ball and Romer (1987a, 1987c). For staggered price setting, see Taylor (1979, 1980), Blanchard (1983, 1986), Ball and Romer (1987b), Okun (1981), and Ball and Cecchetti (1987).

For changes in real wages, see Hall (1986), Rotemberg and Saloner (1986), and Bils (1987). For price rigidity, see McCallum (1986) and Akerlof and Yellen (1985).

16. BMR argue, "Recent progress is largely a result of two innovations in modelling; the introduction of imperfect competition and greater emphasis on price rather than wage rigidities" (p. 13). The introduction of imperfect competition, they also argue, offers six advantages: (1) private costs of rigidity are second order; (2) output is demand determined; (3) booms raise welfare; (4) wage rigidity causes unemployment through low aggregate demand; (5) real wages need not be countercyclical; (6) nominal rigidities have aggregate demand externalities (pp. 13–15).

The second innovation is *product market rigidities,* which offer two advantages. (1) goods are sold in spot markets (in many product markets, buyers clearly operate on their demand curves, so rigidity in the store's prices affects its sales); and (2) Real wages need not be countercyclical (it is easy to explain acyclical or procyclical real wages if prices as well as wages are sticky) (pp. 15–16).

17. I use the same equation numbers as used in the BMR paper for the convenience of reference.

18. BMR argue that "one goal of this model is to redo Lucas's famous analysis and dramatically reinterpret his results" (p. 3).

BMR (pp. 31–32) explain Lucas's imperfect information model (1972) as follows. In Lucas's model, agents wish to change their output in response to changes in their relative prices but not in response to changes in the aggregate price level. When an agent observes a change in his price, he cannot tell whether it results from a relative or an aggregate movement. He acts on his best guess, which is that part of the changes comes from each source. Since agents interpret any price change as partly relative, changes that in fact result from a nominal shock have effects on output. In Lucas's model, the size of the effects of nominal shocks depends on the relative magnitudes of nominal and idiosyncratic real shocks. In particular, if nominal shocks are large, agents attribute most of the movements in their prices to nominal shocks and respond very little. Thus a large variance of nominal aggregate demand leads to a steep Phillips curve. Lucas presents cross-country evidence supporting this prediction in his famous 1973 paper.

However, this explanation is quite different from that of the new Keynesians. BMR provided a Keynesian interpretation of Lucas's results. More variable demand, like high average inflation, leads to more frequent price adjustment. They say that their results are consistent with the Keynesian explanation for the Phillips curve and inconsistent with the classical explanation.

19. A (steady) trend increase in productivity was one of the Kaldor's stylized facts (Refer to "Historical Constancies" in Chapter 3).

20. Refer to note 11 in Chapter 3 for an argument on increasing returns to scale. Wolfe (1968), in which he argues on Kaldor's inaugural lecture (1966b), claims Kaldor's argument on increasing returns to scale in manufacturing industries. Kaldor (1968, p. 389) replies to this, emphasizing that "this is a 'macro-phenomenon' which (in the words of Allyn Young [1928]) 'cannot be discerned adequately by observing the effects of variations in the size of a particular firm or of a particular industry.' " As a growing body of empirical evidence relating to individual industries that tends to confirm its importance, he presents studies of J. S. Bain, C. Pratten and R. M. Dean, J. W. Kendrick, and E. F. Denison (see his p. 389 n. 1 for details).

21. Kaldor (1978, p. xxvii) says that "once we abandon linearity, as we must if we desire to bring abstract theory into a closer approximation to reality, the result is not just that the theory becomes more complicated—as any theory does in the second approximation—but that the whole structure falls to pieces."

22. It is possible to remark on their test regarding estimation of the output-inflation tradeoff. Results for the United Kingdom, the United States, and Japan (BMR, 1988, p. 36, table 4) are as follows:

Country	Data 1948–1972 (1952–1972 for Japan) Tradeoff Parameter τ	Standard Error	Data 1973–1986 (1973–1985 for Japan) Tradeoff Parameter τ	Standard Error
United Kingdom	0.0793	0.1293	−0.0766	0.2197
United States	0.7229	0.0598	0.8486	0.1915
Japan	0.4812	0.1363	0.4119	0.2441
43 countries mean	0.3422	0.1348	0.2761	0.1739

The parameter τ is the coefficient of the change in nominal demand. It is argued that it tells us how much the shock to nominal GNP shows up in output in the first year. If $\tau = 1$, then all of the change in nominal GNP shows up in real GNP; if $\tau = 0$, then all the change in nominal GNP shows up in prices. The result shows that the United States exhibits large effects of aggregate demand on output. However, for the United Kingdom, the tradeoff parameter for 1973 to 1986 is negative, this should be explained. Questions remain.

23. A fallacy of composition is defined as arguing (1) that what is true of each part of a whole is also necessarily true of the whole or (2) that what is true of some parts of a whole is also necessarily true of the whole itself. As such a fallacy is now beginning to be investigated, he presents the studies of Garretsen and Jansen (1989), Bertola and Caballero (1990), and Caballero (1991).

24. We have taken up BMR (1988) as one of the recent representative new Keynesian theories. Dore (1993, sec. 9.4) takes up and discusses "Coordination Failure Through Multiplicity of Agents" as another strand in new Keynesian analysis. He quotes Mankiw and Romer's (1991) definition of new Keynesian economics as directed toward two questions: "the non-neutrality of money and market imperfections as being crucial to the understanding of the macroeconomy. With imperfect markets, there arises the possibility that not all potentially realizable gains will in fact occur. The failure to exploit mutually beneficial trades can be called *coordination failures*" (Dore, pp. 128–129).

This new Keynesian analysis does not use the representative agent, so Dore assesses that this analysis could be potentially rewarding. However, he argues that "there appears to be no systematic attempt to account for the dynamic stylized facts stated in chapter 2. Nor does New Keynesian theory identify a governing mechanism for the cycle as a whole" (p. 132). He points out that the new Keynesians miss an important time dimension of the integral relationship between output, inflation, and unemployment over time, which is shown in his Figure 2.1 (p. 20).

25. See Greenwald and Stiglitz (1988, pp. 251–254, 258–259), Akerlof and Yellen (1985, p. 829), and BMR (1988, p. 10) for an argument on efficient wages.

26. See "Movements of the Labor Share" in Chapter 2. See also note 6 of Chapter 3 for an argument on the accurate real wage rate.

27. Dore (1993, p. 125) argues on this question that "it is commonly perceived that the outcome of the debate on the so-called 'microfoundations of macroeconomics' was that macroeconomics can be done 'properly' only by starting with the behaviour of *micro* units, the household and the firm who are referred to as 'agents.'" Then he quotes Weintraub's (1979, p. 161) conclusion in the survey of microfoundations that the question of what constitutes the appropriate foundations for macroeconomics is an open one. In logic, such a common consent fallacy is called a *consensus gentium fallacy*.

6. CONCLUSIONS

SUMMARY

The purpose of this book has been to explain the changes in specific macroeconomic variables such as the relative share of labor, the profit rate, and the real wage rate in advanced capitalist economies, in relation to the influence of the business cycle in income distribution.

In the pursuit of this inquiry, the economies of three advanced capitalist countries—namely, the United Kingdom, the United States, and Japan—were observed over almost twenty-two years beginning in 1970 and at least three business cycles. The stylized facts were that, first, there is no common feature on whether the labor share moves countercyclically or procyclically in the business cycle. However, with some exceptions, in general the labor share increases in the first year of contraction and decreases in the first year of expansion. Second, the profit rate moves procyclically to the business cycle. The cyclical change of the profit rate does not always coincide with the trough or peak years in the business cycle.

Third, productivity moves procyclically. In particular, a symmetrical change in productivity growth is observed in the business cycle. Productivity (the labor productivity per person employed) increases sharply in the first year of expansion and decreases in the first year of contraction. Fourth, the real wage rate has no common feature, despite the fact that its symmetrical change in the face of the business cycle is clear in the United States. Finally, the two measures of labor shares (with and without labor income from self-employment) are almost similar, though they move differently for some years. Similar movements hold true of the two kinds of estimate of the real wage rate (between the estimates with and without LIS).

In Chapter 2, some of these stylized facts were explained using not an economic model but an economic actor's behavior, the change of economic structure, the change of operating rate of capital, and the features of certain variables. These explanations proved useful, but they are not satisfactory because they are not systematic. For a systematic explanation of the whole economy, a theory or model is necessary.

In this respect, a Kaldorian analysis was attempted. First, Kaldor's model of income distribution (which he called the Keynesian model) was examined, and then two alternative models were applied to an underemployment economy in line with this approach. Two alternatives also examined were the real business cycle (RBC) theory and the new Keynesian theory.

Kaldor's model of income distribution was a full-employment model. According to the Keynesian hypothesis, Kaldor treated the investment/output ratio as an independent variable, which played a strategic role in determining the distributive shares of income. He considered that savings and investment equilibrium will be generated through the change of distributive shares. The thesis of this book concurs with these views.

His model was reformulated by using additional identities and interpreted both in the short run and in the long run. It was shown that (1) Kaldor's model can explain the effect of the change of the investment/output ratio on the relative share of labor, the profit rate on capital, and the real wage rate and (2) the model also can explain, particularly in the short run, an increase in the share of profits leading to an increase of the money wage rate, which in turn results in the high rate of price increase.

However, Kaldor's model has some weaknesses. The first of these results from the background of the model construction. Kaldor recognized three kinds of historical constancies: the relative shares, the capital/output ratio, and the rate of profit on capital. However, actual results were rather negative with respect to these constancies. Second, among various comments on Kaldor's model, one of the strongest criticisms is that his model cannot explain the distribution of income in an underemployment economy. This is due to the fact that his equation, which explains the distributive share, has two unknown variables in relation to underemployment.

Many writers of the Keynesian persuasion have introduced the first postulate of the classical theory (based on the marginal productivity principle) and completed a model encompassing underemployment. However, alternative ways to complete it as a macroeconomic model along Kaldor's line, without introducing this first postulate, were considered here. The first alternative way was to introduce an equation in which the volume of the labor force employed was determined by the volume of investment (equation (4) in Chapter

4). This was called an *employment-decision approach*. The other alternative was to introduce a kind of markup pricing equation based on full-cost principles, which we called a markup pricing approach (equation (4a) in Chapter 4). These alternative models are in line with Kaldor's standpoint, in the sense that investment is treated as an independent variable and the marginal productivity principle is not involved. They are constructed in both nominal and gross terms, which is a departure from Kaldor's original model.

The first model (Model A, the employment-decision model) had the possibility of explaining, more or less, the countercyclical change of the labor share to the business cycle, and the procyclical change of both the profit rate and labor productivity. Therefore, this model explains most of the stylized facts presented in Chapter 2.

However, the model has some weaknesses. First, this is a simple model. To explain the symmetrical change of both the labor share and productivity growth in a more refined way, a more specified model is needed. Second, the model is constructed for the short run, and its properties examined through the use of comparative statics. This model should be developed to encompass the long run.

The second model (Model B, the markup pricing model) can possibilly explain procyclical changes of the labor share, the profit rate, the real wage rate, and labor productivity. This model also explains some stylized facts regarding profit rate and productivity.

However, this model has more weaknesses than the first. The model shares the two similar weaknesses possessed by Model A. It has a fundamental feature related to the procyclical change of the labor share, which depends on the markup pricing equation. With regard to this point, it is arguably safe to say that the markup price rule will be observed in oligopolistic industries, but this rule should be tested as to whether or not it is applicable to the whole economy.

The RBC theory is the latest incarnation of the classical view of economic fluctuations. RBC models deal with "the idealized state of dynamic equilibrium" argued by Hicks (1933), which gives us a way of assessing the extent or degree of disequilibrium and also some norms for policy targets. In these respects, this approach may be useful. However, there were weaknesses that might cause us to discard the usefulness of the models.

First, the RBC theory embraces the classical dichotomy, but when we admit the inflexibility of wages and prices, keeping faith with the classical dichotomy presents difficulties. For example, it may not be plausible for economists of the classical approach to assume that fluctuations in employment are fully voluntary, particularly during a recession. Second, they explain fluctuations by exogenous disturbances such as technological change, which should be explained endogenously. Solow's residual, calculated by the Cobb-Douglas production function, on which RBC models follow, does not seem to provide proper evidence regarding exogenous technological disturbances. Third, the equilibrium growth model needs a broad set of conditions to have steady-state growth, but these are not always plausible: the conditions are

(1) per capita values converging to constants at an equal growth rate and (2) labor-augmenting or Harrod-neutral technological progress. Therefore, the RBC theory is weak in explaining actual growth paths, particularly the change of variables in the labor market. It has difficulty in explaining the changes of the relative share of labor and of labor productivity.

The new Keynesian theory is also the latest development of the Keynesian theory. Ball, Mankiw, and Romer's paper (1988) was examined as being representative of this theory. BMR provided microeconomic foundations for nominal rigidities by introducing optimizing behavior. Two innovations—the introduction of imperfect competition and product market rigidities—contributed greatly to the development of the model.

However, the BMR model has some weaknesses. First, their treatment of price setting based on optimizing behavior does not seem to be plausible. They assume that an equal proportion of firms changes prices reflecting BMR's expected price change rule at every instant, but this presents difficulties in some phases of the business cycle, especially in the slump. Second, the model has difficulty in explaining the change of productivity in the business cycle, particularly in the contraction years. Third, it is clear that the profit-maximization principle has difficulty in explaining the observed trend increase in productivity due to technological progress and increasing returns to scale in a macroeconomy.

The new Keynesian theory also has difficulty in explaining the change of variables in the labor market. It can possibilly explain procyclical movements of the profit rate but has difficulty in explaining the changes of the relative share of labor and productivity as discussed in Chapter 5.

Finally, both theories need to reply to the criticism on methodology presented by the recent investigations that the representative agent framework leads to a fallacy of composition.

METHODOLOGICAL RESEARCH AGENDA

The development and testing of a theory in economics can take many forms. Econometric investigation is only one form. The proponents of the RBC use the method of model calibration as an alternative. However, a first step to model testing requires a statement of a research agenda for future work. Three methodological research agenda are examined briefly in the following order—determinants of investment, government policy and international trade, and test of the models and model calibration.

Determinants of Investment

The Keynesian model deals with investment as an independent variable. This treatment is important. However, how is it determined? Robinson (1960a, p. 146) argues on the determinants of the ratio of investment to the value of total output that

The rate of investment in turn can be accounted for in two ways which do not seem to be connected with each other. Investment is determined, in one sense, by profit expectations, the "animal spirits" [Keynes, 1936, p. 161] of entrepreneurs which include them to take the risks of investment, and the state of supply of finance, which may be subsumed under the head of the level of interest rates.

In another sense, the rate of investment that can be maintained over long run depends on technical conditions and the supply of labour.

Following Robinson, further inquiries are needed. First, entrepreneurs' attitude towards investment are heavily driven by "animal spirits," a phrase introduced by Keynes and subsequently stressed by Joan Robinson. These are often different from country to country and from time to time. This begs a more complex analysis including anthropological and sociological factors.

Second, later on neo-Keynesians developed their research to the state of supply of finance.[1] Without sufficient financing, entrepreneurs cannot carry on their planned investment, in which depreciation and cash-flow play important roles.

Third, the rate of investment in the long run relates to Harrod's "natural rate of growth," as Robinson refers to it. The discussion on the real forces of population growth and technological progress should be incorporated in the growth model.

All these questions are important because the Keynesian hypothesis on investment is a key factor in Kaldorian models. These inquiries are left as a subject for future research.

Government Policy and International Trade

Regarding Model A (Employment-Decision Approach)

If we take investment I as

Gross capital formation + Current balance in balance of payment accounts,

it is possible for Model A to deal with both government policy and international trade. Corresponding to this treatment of I, the savings propensity out of profits is estimated as

$$s_p = \frac{\text{Total savings} - \text{Savings from wages (and salaries)}}{\text{GNP} - \text{Labor income}},$$

where

Savings from wages = $s_w \times$ Labor income.

This s_p is not restricted to corporate savings but now refers to a broader measure.[2]

Gross capital formation includes capital formation by government. Government investment makes up I as a whole. The current balance also makes up total investment. So the surplus on the account shows positive investment, and the deficit shows negative investment. According to whether the government policy and the international trade increase total investment or not, we would be able to show the effects of these on the relative share, the profit rate, and the real wage rate by the model.

Regarding Model B (Markup Pricing Approach)

By equations (1) and (4a) we obtain markup rate r:

$$r = \frac{P - D}{W + D}.$$

If we take total output Y as GNP and define the profits P in a broad sense that includes indirect taxes less subsidies, then the markup rate is distorted by government policies on both indirect taxes and subsidies. However, if we take Y as NI (national income excluding indirect taxes less subsidies), government policies on these are outside our model, and these policies would not directly affect any variable in the model. International trade is a distorting factor to markup pricing in any case above (GNP and NI), especially in the imbalance on current account.

Test of the Models and Model Calibration

Model A consists of five identities and two equations, the latter of which are supported by the stylized facts by Dore (1993). For the test of the model, some given variables are directly obtained from macro data (or survey data), and the others may be separately estimated by one way or another. The average propensity to save out of profits may be obtained by the way presented above. For I^*, it needs some formulation. When we get I^*, we obtain values a and b, and c and h by regression, respectively.

For Model B, exogenous variables are directly obtained from or estimated by macro data (or survey data). Feeding these into the model results in unknown variables. For a more plausible test, productivity is an endogenous variable by adding equation (5a), for example.

An alternative strategy called *calibration*[3] also should be employed. The observations presented here are restricted to twenty-two years, though some of these are supported by other investigations covering longer periods. These observations are not sufficient to support our findings. However, calibration makes it possible not only to complement empirical data but also to mimic the data generating process.

For the model calibration, investment is predetermined,[4] then coefficients are obtained from national statistics and survey data, and finally we simulate to test the model. If one of these models is successful as a result of the test, it would provide a clue about predicting some features of the business cycle.

QUESTIONS REMAINING FOR THE FUTURE

Each model discussed here has its usefulness and weaknesses. However, judging from our inquiry into explaining the changes of macroeconomic variables in the business cycle, Kaldorian models are fairly effective. Among others, the employment-decision approach (Model A) should be able to explain most of our stylized facts.

However, as was discussed earlier in this conclusion, this model had two weaknesses: it is a simple model and is discussed in the short run. Some questions remain regarding further development of this model.

First is the test of the model. Our analysis was basically on the theoretical level, giving logical reasoning. Although to some extent our arguments were based on some stylized facts, the model itself is not tested. Among others, employment-related function (4) and productivity-related function (5) in the model, both of which concur with Dore's stylized facts, should be specified further. The idea that the volume of employment relates to investment may be basically acceptable, but it should be tested as to the degree an investment change effects the change of employment. Then, the idea that productivity relates to the volume of employment may be acceptable, but it should also be tested as to the degree productivity depends on the change of employment. Through these tests, we would have a clue to constructing more specified equations and then a more elaborate model.

Next is the treatment of the money wage rate. Kaldorian models fundamentally depend on both changes of investment and money wages. Investment may be treated as a policy variable, but money wages are fairly difficult to deal with in the same way. We can discuss the determinants of money wages. If it is possible to add a money wages function to the model, the model has greater potential for elaborate predictions of the economy.

Third, our arguments are restricted to the short run, and the models should be extended to the long-run model. In this respect, Goodwin (1967) would be one of the important examples.[5] For Goodwin's growth model is the first model to achieve successful integration of growth into the cycle model. According to Dore (1993, p. 216), the model "explicitly puts the issue of income distribution at the centre of the explanation of the business cycle" and "explains all but one of the set of ten stylized facts."[6] Furthermore, we consider that model calibration is useful, which makes it possible to complement empirical data and to mimic the data-generating process as explained in the preceding section.

Finally, if these investigations can be done successfully, we could fully develop our arguments in relation to policy relevance. We have not had a systematic policy influencing functional distribution, though it is considered in general that some policies bring full employment and keep prices stable and that some industrial policies relate to this.[7] But this is a complex investigation. However, I believe our Kaldorian approach has the potential for dealing with this problem and contributing to the argument.[8]

NOTES

1. See Kaldor (1966a) and Wood (1975), for example.

Kaldor (1966a) clarifies the reasons that the savings propensity out of profits must be very considerably greater than the savings propensity out of wages and salaries, or of household incomes in general. He attaches great importance to the notion of internal finance that consists of depreciation and retained profits, and obtains a neo-Pasinetti theorem based on equilibrium in the securities market.

However, in recent years, a greater importance is attached to the availability of credit, which is relevant to investment behaviour (as well as in the field of corporate finance) than to the rate of interest (see Jaffee and Stiglitz, 1990).

2. Following this treatment, Iyoda (1980a, 1980b, 1982) estimates the relative share and the real wage rate, which is the first case applying Kaldor's model of income distribution to an actual economy. Iyoda (1980b) is a brief summarization of previous papers (1979, 1980a).

3. Plosser (1989, pp. 70–71) points out two examples of calibration, explaining the strategy. Kydland and Prescott (1982) made popular this technique, and Balland, Shoven, and Whalley (1985) employed it more widely in the applied general equilibrium.

4. For example, the following formula can be employed:

$$I_t = \alpha I_{t-1} + \beta I_{t-2} + \varepsilon_t,$$

where

ε = error term.

The Values of α and β can be imputed to mimic the deterministic path of investment in each economy.

5. When I met Professor Anthony B. Atkinson to discuss my dissertation in January 1994, he recommended Goodwin's works.

6. Refer to note 26 of Chapter 2 for an argument on Dore's stylized facts, among which his stylized fact (3) that "procyclical real wages indicating that the wage share out of national income is also procyclical" (Dore, 1993, p. 19) can be challenged.

7. Financial and monetary policies that aim at full employment, price stability, and efficiency of resource allocation are considered as related policies to functional distribution in a broad sense. Other related policies are industrial policies that promote competition and guard or support particular industries. See Planning Bureau of the Economic Planning Agency (Japan) (1975, pp. 105–107) for a discussion relating to this.

8. Iyoda (1971a) argued about incomes policy by Kaldor's model of income distribution, though the argument was subject to full employment. Then Iyoda (1976, 1978) also discussed policy relevance in a one-sector model (1976) and a two-sector extension (1978), respectively. We could find some interesting policy implications, but these models have the same weakness that was presented in "Introduction" of Chapter 4. Iyoda (1982) argued on functional distribution policies from Kaldorian view by considering his (Iyoda) estimates of Japanese relative share of labour and the real wage rate (1979, 1980a, 1980b).

REFERENCES

Note: An asterisk (*) after title indicates in Japanese.

Akerlof, George A., Andrew Rose, and Janet Yellen. (1988). "Comments." *Brookings Papers on Economic Activity* 1, 66–75.

Akerlof, George A., and Janet L. Yellen. (1985). "A Near-Rational Model of the Business Cycle, with Wage and Price Inertia." *Quarterly Journal of Economics* (supplement) 100, 823–838.

Atsumi, Hiroshi. (1960). "Mr. Kaldor's Theory of Income Distribution." *Review of Economic Studies* 73, 109–118.

Ball, Laurence, and Stephen G. Cecchetti. (1987). "Imperfect Information and Staggered Price Setting." Working Paper 2201, NBER.

Ball, Laurence, N. Gregory Mankiw, and David Romer. (1988). "The New Keynesian Economics and the Output-Inflation Trade-Off (with Comments and Discussion)." *Brookings Papers on Economic Activity* 1, 1–65 (66–82).

Ball, Laurence, and David Romer. (1987a). "Are Prices Too Sticky?" Working Paper 2171, NBER.

Ball, Laurence, and David Romer. (1987b). "The Equilibrium and Optimal Timing of Price Changes." Working Paper 2412, NBER.

Ball, Laurence, and David Romer. (1987c). "Real Rigidities and the Non-Neutrality of Money." Working Paper 2476, NBER.

Ballard, Charles L., John V. Shoven, and John Whalley. (1985). "General Equilibrium Computations on the Marginal Welfare Costs of Taxes in the United States." *American Economic Review* 75, 128–138.

Barro, Robert J., and Herschel I. Grossman. (1971). "A General Disequilibrium Model of Income and Employment." *American Economic Review* 61, 82–93.

Bertola, Giuseppe, and Ricardo J. Caballero. (1990). "Kinked Adjustment Costs and Aggregate Dynamics." *NBER Macroeconomics Annual 1990*, 237–288.

Bils, Mark J. (1985). "Real Wages over the Business Cycle: Evidence from Panel Data." *Journal of Political Economy* 93, 666–689.

Bils, Mark J. (1987). "Cyclical Pricing of Durable Luxuries." Working Paper 83, University of Rochester Centre for Economic Research.

Blanchard, Olivier J. (1983). "Price Asynchronization and Price Level Inertia." in Rudiger Dornbush and Mario Henrique Simonsen (eds.). *Inflation, Debt, and Indexation* (pp. 3–24). London: MIT Press.
Blanchard, Olivier J. (1986). "The Wage Price Spiral." *Quarterly Journal of Economics* 101, 543–565.
Blanchard, Olivier J., and Nobuhiro Kiyotaki. (1987). "Monopolistic Competition and the Effects of Aggregate Demand." *American Economic Review* 77, 647–666.
Bodkin, Ronald J. (1969). "Real Wages and Cyclical Variations in Employment: A Reexamination of the Evidence." *Canadian Journal of Economics* 2(1), 353–374.
Brainard, William C., and George L. Perry. (1988). "Editors Summary." *Brookings Papers on Economic Activity* 1, ix–xxxiii.
Brown, E. H. Phelps, and Peter E. Hart. (1952). "The Share of Wages in the National Income." *Economic Journal* 246, 253–277.
Brown, E. H. Phelps, and Bernard Weber. (1953). "Accumulation, Productivity and Distribution in the British Economy, 1870–1938." *Economic Journal* 250, 263–288.
Caballero, Ricardo J. (1991). "A Fallacy of Composition." National Bureau of Economic Research, Working Paper Series 3735.
Caplin, Andrew S., and Daniel F. Spulber. (1987). "Menu Costs and the Neutrality of Money." *Quarterly Journal of Economics* 102, 703–725. Reprinted in N. Gregory Mankiw and David Romer (eds.) (1991), *New Keynesian Economics* (vol. 1). Cambridge, MA: MIT Press.
Chamberlin, Edward Hastings. (1933). *The Theory of Monopolistic Competition*. Cambridge, MA: Harvard University Press.
Domar, Evsey D. (1961). "The Capital-Output Ratio in the United States: Its Variation and Stability." In Friedrich Lutz and Douglas C. Hague (eds.), *The Theory of Capital* (pp. 95–117). London: Macmillan.
Dore, Mohammed H. I. (1993). *The Macrodynamics of Business Cycles: A Comparative Evaluation*. Oxford: Blackwell.
Dunlop, John T. (1938). "The Movement of Real and Money Wage Rates." *Economic Journal* 48, 413–434.
Economic Planning Agency. (1977). *Economic Survey of Japan 1975–1976*. Tokyo: The Japan Times.
Economic Planning Agency. (1993). *Economic Survey of Japan 1991–1992*. Tokyo: Printing Bureau, Ministry of Finance.
Everitt, Brian S. (1977). *The Analysis of Contingency Tables*. London: Chapman and Hall.
Feldstein, Martin S., and Lawrence H. Summers. (1977). "Is the Rate of Profit Falling?" *Brookings Paper on Economic Activity* 1, 211–228.
Fellner, William John. (1947). *Monetary Policies and Full Employment* (2nd ed.). Berkeley: University of California Press.
Findlay, Ronald. (1960). "Economic Growth and the Distributive Shares." *Review of Economic Studies* 74, 167–178.
Fischer, Stanley. (1977). "Long-Term Contracts, Rational Expectations and the Optimal Money Supply Rule." *Journal of Political Economy* 85, 191–205.
Friedman, Milton. (1968). "The Role of Monetary Policy." *American Economic Review* 58, 1–17.
Garretsen, Harry, and Maarten C. W. Janssen. (1989). "Two Fallacies of Composition in a Keynesian OLG Model." University of Croningen Research Memorandum 317.
Gearly, Patrick T., and John Kennan. (1982). "The Employment-Real Wage Relationship: An International Study." *Journal of Political Economy* 90, 854–871.
Goodwin, Richard M. (1967). "A Growth Cycle." In Charles H. Feinstein (ed.), *Socialism, Capitalism and Economic Growth: Essays Presented to Maurice Dobb* (pp. 54–58). Cambridge: Cambridge University Press.
Gray, Jo Anna. (1978). "On Indexation and Contract Length." *Journal of Political Economy* 86, 1–18.
Greenwald, Bruce C., and Joseph E. Stiglitz. (1988). "Examining Alternative Macroeconomic Theories (with Comments and discussion)." *Brookings Papers on Economic Activity* 1, 207–260 (261–270).
Hahnell, Robin, and Howard J. Sherman. (1982). "Income Distribution on the Business Cycle: Three Conflicting Hypotheses." *Journal of Economic Issues* 16(1), 49–73.
Hall, Robert E. (1986). "Market Structure and Macroeconomic Fluctuations." *BPEA* 2, 285–322.
Harrod, Roy F. (1948). *Towards a Dynamic Economics*. London: Macmillan.

Hicks, John. (1933). "Equilibrium and the Cycle." Reprinted in John Hicks, *Collected Essays on Economic Theory* (1982), *Vol. 2, Money, Interest and Wages* (pp. 28–41). Oxford: Basil Blackwell.
Hicks, John. (1939). *Value and Capital*. London: Oxford University Press.
Hicks, John. (1965). *Capital and Growth*. New York: Oxford University Press.
Iyoda, Mitsuhiko. (1971a). "An Application of Prof. N. Kaldor's Distribution Model to an Argument on Incomes Policy."* *Journal of Economics* (Osaka City University) 65(4), 128–141.
Iyoda, Mitsuhiko. (1971b). "Memorandum: On Prof. N. Kaldor's Distribution Theory and Growth Theory." *Osaka City University Economic Review* 7, 35–53.
Iyoda, Mitsuhiko. (1975). "Implication of Kaldorian Theory of Distribution: In Comparison with Neoclassical Theory of Distribution."* *Economic and Business Review* (St. Andrew's University, Osaka) 17(1), 29–41.
Iyoda, Mitsuhiko. (1976). "An Application of Kaldorian Model of Income Distribution to an Under-employment Economy (1)."* *Economic and Business Review* (St. Andrew's University) 18(2), 1–12.
Iyoda, Mitsuhiko. (1978). "An Application of Kaldorian Model of Income Distribution to an Under-employment Economy (2): A Two Sector Model."* *Economic and Business Review* (St. Andrew's University) 20(2), 1–14.
Iyoda, Mitsuhiko. (1979). "Estimation of Relative Income Shares in Postwar Japan."* *Bulletin of Research Institute* (St. Andrew's University, Osaka) 4(2), 23–32.
Iyoda, Mitsunhiko. (1980a). "The Fluctuation of Relative Income Shares and the Real Wage Rate in Postwar Japan."* *Bulletin of Research Institute* (St. Andrew's University) 5(2), 1–12.
Iyoda, Mitsuhiko. (1980b). "The Fluctuation of Relative Income Shares and the Real Wage Rate in Postwar Japan." *International Review of Economics and Business* (Bocconi University, Italy) 27 (7–8), 665–682.
Iyoda, Mitsuhiko. (1982). "An Examination of Functional Distribution Policies."* In Kazuo Mazane, Hisao Onoe, and Shinji Shibayama (eds.), *State and Market System* (pp. 204–220). Kyoto: Mineruba Shobo.
Iyoda, Mitsuhiko. (1984). "A Comparative Study of the Self-employed Businesses Between Japan and the U.K., 1950–82."* *Economic and Business Review* (St. Andrew's University, Osaka) 26(1), 55–83.
Iyoda, Mitsuhiko. (1985). "Estimation of Relative Shares of Labour in Postwar U.K." *Bulletin of Research Institute* (St. Andrew's University, Osaka) 11(2), 39–51.
Iyoda, Mitsuhiko. (1987). "Estimation of Relative Income Shares of Labour in Postwar Japan, 1950–85."* *Bulletin of Research Institute* (St. Andrew's University, Osaka) 13(2), 1–10.
Iyoda, Mitsuhiko. (1988). "Structural Changes in the Economy and Unincorporated Enterprises: A Comparison Between Japan, the U.K. and (South) Korea."* *Bulletin of Research Institute* (St. Andrew's University, Osaka) 14(1), 19–35.
Jaffee, Dwight, and Joseph Stigliz. (1990). "Credit Rationing." In Benjamin M. Friedman and Frank H. Hahn (eds.), *Handbook of Monetary Economics*. (vol. 2, pp. 837–888). Amsterdam: Elsevier Science.
Johansen, Leif. (1960). *A Multi-Sectoral Study of Economic Growth*. Amsterdam: North-Holland.
Kaldor, Nicholas. (1955–1956). "Alternative Theories of Distribution." *Review of Economic Studies* 23(2), 83–100. Reprinted in Nicholas Kaldor (1960), *Essays on Value and Distribution* (pp. 209–236). London: Duckworth. (Quoted pages are from the *Essays*.)
Kaldor, Nicholas. (1957a). "Capitalist Evolution in the Light of Keynesian Economics." *Sankhyā* (May). Reprinted in Nicholas Kaldor (1960), *Essays on Economic Stability and Growth* (pp. 243–258). London: Duckworth. (Quoted pages are from the *Essays*.)
Kaldor, Nicholas. (1957b). "A Model of Economic Growth." *Economic Journal* 268, 591–624. Reprinted in Nicholas Kaldor (1960), *Essays on Economic Stability and Growth* (pp. 259–300). London: Duckworth. (Quoted pages are from the *Essays*.)
Kaldor , Nicholas,. (1960a). "A Rejoinder to Mr. Atsumi and Professor Tobin." *Review of Economic Studies* 73, 121–123.
Kaldor, Nicholas. (1960b). "A Rejoinder to Mr. Findlay." *Review of Economic Studies* 74, 179–181.
Kaldor, Nicholas. (1961). "Capital Accumulation and Economic Growth." In Friedrich A. Lutz and Douglas C. Hague (eds.), *The Theory of Capital* (pp. 177–222). London: Macmillan.
Kaldor, Nicholas. (1966a). "Marginal Productivity and the Macro-Economic Theories of Distribution: Comment on Samuelson and Modigliani." *Review of Economic Studies* 96, 309–319.

Kaldor, Nicholas. (1966b). *Causes of the Slow Rate of Economic Growth of the United Kingdom.* Cambridge: Cambridge University Press.
Kaldor, Nicholas. (1968). "Productivity and Growth in Manufacturing Industry: A Reply." *Economica* 140, 385–391.
Kaldor, Nicholas. (1978). "Introduction." In Nicholas Kaldor, *Further Essays on Economic Theory* (pp. vii–xxix). London: Duckworth.
Kalecki, Michal. (1942). "A Theory of Profits." *Economic Journal* 206–207, 258–267.
Kalecki, Michal. (1954). *Theory of Economic Dynamics.* London: Unwin University Books.
Keane, Michael, Robert Moffitt, and David Runkle. (1988). "Real Wages over the Business Cycle: Estimating the Impact of Heterogeneity with Micro Data." *Journal of Political Economy* 96, 1232–1266.
Keynes, John Maynard. (1930). *A Treatise on Money. Vol. 1 The Pure Theory of Money.* London: Macmillan. (Quotations are from *The Collected Writings of John Maynard Keynes* (vol. 5), Cambridge: Cambridge Printing House, 1971.)
Keynes, John Maynard. (1936). *The General Theory of Employment, Interest and Money.* London: Macmillan.
King, Robert G., Charles I. Plosser, and Sergio Rebelo. (1988). "Production, Growth and Business Cycles II, New Directions." *Journal of Monetary Economics* 21, 309–341.
King, Robert G., Charles I. Plosser, James Stock, and Mark Watson. (1987). "Stochastic Trends and Economic Fluctuations." Rochester Centre for Economic Research, Working Paper 79.
King, John, and Philip Regan. (1976). *Relative Income Shares.* London: Macmillan.
King, Robert G., and Sergio Rebelo. (1986). "Business Cycles with Endogenous Growth." Unpublished manuscript, University of Rochester.
King, Robert G., and Sergio Rebelo. (1988). "Public Policy and Economic Growth." Unpublished working paper, University of Rochester.
Kravis, Irving B. (1959). "Relative Income Shares in Fact and Theory." *American Economic Review* 49(5), 917–949.
Kuh, Edwin. (1960). "Profits, Profit Markups and Productivity." Study Paper 15, Joint Economic Committee, Washington, DC.
Kuh, Edwin. (1963). "Income Distribution Over the Business Cycle." Unpublished paper.
Kuznets, Simon. (1952). "Long Term Changes in the National Income of the U.S.A. Since 1970." In Simon Kuznets (ed.), *Income and Wealth, Series II.* Cambridge: Bowes and Bowes.
Kuznets, Simon. (1966). *Mondern Economic Growth: Rate, Structure and Spread.* New Haven: Yale University Press.
Kydland, Finn E., and Edward C. Prescott. (1982). "Time to Build and Aggregate Fluctuations." *Econometrica* 50, 1345–1370.
Long, John B., and Charles I. Plosser. (1983). "Real Business Cycles." *Journal of Political Economy* 91, 1345–1370.
Lucas, Robert E., Jr. (1972). "Expectations and the Neutrality of Money." *Journal of Economic Theory* 4, 103–124.
Lucas, Robert E., Jr. (1973). "Some International Evidence on Output-Inflation Tradeoffs." *American Economic Review* 63, 326–334.
Lucas, Robert E., Jr. (1976). "Economic Policy Evaluation: A Critique." *Carnegie-Rochester Conference Series on Public Policy* 1, 19–46.
Lucas, Robert, Jr. (1980). "Methods and Problems in Business Cycle Theory." *Journal of Money, Credit and Banking* 12, 696–715.
Lucas, Robert, Jr. (1988). "On the Mechanics of Economic Development." *Journal of Monetary Economics* 22, 3–42.
Lutz, Friedrich. (1961). "Introduction." In Friedrich A. Lutz and Douglas C. Hague (eds.), *The Theory of Capital* (pp. ix–xiii). London: Macmillan.
MaCallum, Bennett T. (1986). "On 'Real' and 'Sticky-Price' Theories of the Business Cycle." *Journal of Money, Credit, and Banking* 18, 397–414.
Malinvaud, Edmond. (1977). *The Theory of Unemployment Reconsidered.* Oxford: Basil Blackwell.
Mankiw, N. Gregory. (1985). "Small Menu Costs and Large Business Cycles: A Macroeconomic Model of Monopoly." *Quarterly Journal of Economics* 100, 529–537.
Mankiw, N. Gregory. (1989). "Real Business Cycles: A New Keynesian Perspective." *Journal of Economic Perspectives* 3(3), 79–90.
Mankiw, N. Gregory, and David Romer (eds.). (1991). *New Keynesian Economics.* Cambridge, MA: MIT Press.

Matthews, Kent. (1994). "Review on Dore (Mohammed H. I.) *The Macrodynamics of Business Cycles: A Comparative Evaluation*, and Mullineux (Andy), Dickinson (David G.), and Peng (WenSheng) *Business Cycles: Theory and Evidence.*" *Economic Journal* 426, 1206–1209.

Matthews, Kent, and Patrick Minford. (1987). "Mrs Thatcher's Economic Policies 1979–87." *Economic Policy* 5, 57–101.

Maywald, K. (1956). "Fire Insurance and the Capital Coefficient in Great Britain 1866–1952." *Economic History Review* (2nd ser.) 9(1), 89–105.

Meade, James E. (1960). A *Neo-classical Theory of Economic Growth.* London: George Allen and Unwin.

Moore, Geoffrey H. (1969). "Forecasting Short-Term Economic Change." *Journal of the American Statistical Association* 64, 1–22. Reprinted in National Bureau of Economic Research (ed.) (1983), *Business Cycles, Inflation, and Forecasting* (NBER Studies in Business Cycles No. 24) (2nd ed.) (pp. 401–432). Cambridge, MA: Ballinger. (Quoted pages are from this reprint.)

Muellbauer, John. (1986). "Productivity and Competitiveness in British Manufacturing." *Oxford Review of Economic Policy* 2(3), i–xxv.

Neftci, Salih N. (1978). "A Time-Series Analysis of the Real Wages-Employment Relationship." *Journal of Political Economy* 86, 281–291.

Neild, Robert R. (1963). *Pricing and Employment in the Trade Cycle.* Cambridge: Cambridge University Press.

Nelson, Charles R., and Charles I. Plosser. (1982). "Trends and Random Walks in Macroeconomic Time Series: Some Evidence and Implications." *Journal of Monetary Economics* 10, 139–167.

Okamoto, Takeyuki. (1967). "The Neo-classical and the Keynesaian Theories of Distribution."* *Journal of Economic Studies* (School of Economics, University of Osaka Prefecture) 46, 338–321.

Okamoto, Takeyuki. (1981). *Macro Economics on Employment and [Income] Distribution.** Tokyo: Yuhikaku.

Okun, Arthur M. (1962). "Potential GNP: Its Measurement and Significance." *Proceedings of the Business and Economic Statistic Section* (pp. 98–103), American Statistical Association. Reprinted in Arthur M. Okun (1970), *The Political Economy of Prosperity.* Washington, DC: Brookings Institution.

Okun, Arthur M. (1981). *Prices and Quantities: A Macro Economic Analysis.* Washington, DC: Brookings Institution.

Pasinetti, Luigi L. (1962). "Rate of Profit and Income Distribution in Relation to the Rate of Economic Growth." *Review of Economic Studies* 81, 267–279.

Pasinetti, Luigi L. (1966). "New Results in an Old Framework: Comment on Samuelson and Modigliani." *Review of Economic studies* 96, 303–306.

Patinkin, Don. (1956). *Money, Interest and Prices: An Integration of Monetary and Value Theory.* Evanston, IL: Row, Peterson.

Planning Bureau of the Economic Planning Agency (Japan). (1975). *Realities and Questions of the Distribution of Property and Income.** Tokyo: Ministry of Finance Printing Bureau.

Plosser, Charles I. (1989). "Understanding Real Business Cycles." *Journal of Economic Perspectives* 3(3), 51–77.

Raisian, John. (1983). "Contracts, Job Experience and Cyclical Labour Market Adjustments." *Journal of Labour Economics* 1(2), 152–170.

Ricardo, David. (1817). *On the Principles of Political Economy and Taxation.* London: John Murray. (Quotations are from Piero Sraffa (ed.) (1953), *The Works and Correspondence of David Ricardo* (vol. 1). Cambridge: Cambridge University Press).

Robinson, Joan. (1952). *The Rate of Interest and Other Essays.* London: Macmillan. Reprinted (1979) under the title *The Generalization of the General Theory and Other Essays*, London: Macmillan.

Robinson, Joan. (1953–1954). "The Production Function and the Theory of Capital." *Review of Economic Studies* 55, 81–106. Reprinted in Joan Robinson (1960), *Collected Economic Papers* (vol. 2) (pp. 114–131). Oxford: Basil Blackwell.

Robinson, Joan. (1956). *The Accumulation of Capital.* London: Macmillan.

Robinson, Joan. (1960a). "The Theory of Distribution." In Joan Robinson, *Collected Economic Papers* (vol. 2) (pp. 145–158). Oxford: Basil Blackwell. (An amended version of a paper published in French in *Économie Appliqué*, October-December 1957).

Robinson, Joan. (1960b). *Exercises in Economic Analysis.* London: Macmillan.

Robinson, Joan. (1966). "Comment on Samuelson and Modigliani." *Review of Economic Studies* 96, 307–308.

Robinson, Joan. (1967). "Marginal Productivity." *Indian Economic Review* 2(1), 75–83. Reprinted in Joan Robinson (1973), *Collected Economic Papers* (vol. 4) (pp. 129–138). Oxford: Basil Blackwell.

Romer, Paul. (1986). "Increasing Returns and Long Run Growth." *Journal of Political Economy* 94, 1002–1073.

Rotemberg, Julio J., and Garth Saloner. (1986). "A Supergame-Theoretic Model of Price Wars During Booms." *American Economic Review* 76, 390–407.

Samuelson, Paul A., and Franco Modigliani. (1966a). "The Pasinetti Paradox in Neoclassical and More General Models." *Review of Economic Studies* 96, 269–301.

Samuelson, Paul A., and Franco Modigliani. (1966b). "Reply to Pasinetti and Robinson." *Review of Economic Studies* 96, 321–330.

Sargent, Thomas J. (1978). "Estimation of Dynamic Labour Demand Schedules Under Rational Expectations." *Journal of Political Economy* 86, 1009–1044.

Sen, Amartya K. (1963). "Neo-Classical and Neo-Keynesian Theories of Distribution." *Economic Record* 85, 53–64.

Sims, Christfer A. (1988). "Comments." *Brookings Papers on Economic Activity* 1, 75–79.

Solow, Robert M. (1956). "A Contribution to the Theory of Economic Growth." *Quarterly Journal of Economics* 70, 65–94.

Solow, Robert M. (1957). "Technical Change and the Aggregate Production Function." *Review of Economic Studies* 39, 312–320.

Solow, Robert M. (1966). "Distribution in the Long and Short Run." In Jean Marchal and Bernard Durco (eds.), *The Distribution of National Income* (pp. 449–475). London: Macmillan.

Spencer, Peter. (1987). *Britain's Productivity Renaissance* (CSFB Economics). London: Credit Suisse First Boston, (June).

Spencer, Peter. (1988). *Britain's Productivity Renaissance: An Update*. London: *Shearson Lehman Hutton* (December).

Swan, Trevor W. (1956). "Economic Growth and Capital Accumulation." *Economic Record* 32, 334–361.

Tarshis, Lorie. (1939). "Changes in Real and Money Wage Rates." *Economic Journal* 49, 150–154.

Taylor, John B. (1979). "Staggered Wage Setting in a Macro Model." *American Economic Review* 69, 108–113 (Papers and Proceedings, 1978).

Taylor, John B. (1980). "Aggregate Dynamics and Staggered Contracts." *Journal of Political Economy* 88, 1–23.

Tobin, James. (1960). "Towards a General Kaldorian Theory of Distribution." *Review of Economic Studies* 73, 119–120.

Uzawa, Hirofumi. (1965). "Optimum Technical Change in an Aggregative Model of Economic Growth." *International Economic Review* 6, 18–31.

Watanabe, Hiromu. (1960). "On the Recent Keynesian Theory of Income Distribution."* *Doshisha University Economic Review* 10(3–4), 22–26.

Watanabe, Hiromu. (1969). "The Short-run Theory of Macro-Distribution and Trade Unions."* *Doshisha University Economic Review* 18(1/2/3), 172–197. Reprinted in Hiromu Watanabe (1979), *Capital Accumulation and Income Distribution** (pp. 3–23). Tokyo: Yuhikaku.

Watanabe, Hiromu. (1979). *Capital Accumulation and Income Distribution.** Tokyo: Yuhikaku.

Weintraub, E. Roy. (1979). *Microfoundations: The Compatibility of Microeconomics and Macroeconomics*. Cambridge: Cambridge University Press.

Weintraub, Sidney. (1958). *An Approach to the Theory of Income Distribution*. Philadelphia: Chilton.

Wolfe, James N. (1968). "Productivity and Growth in Manufacturing Industry: Some Reflections on Professor Kaldor's Inaugural Lecture." *Economica* 138, 117–126.

Wood, Adrian. (1975). *A Theory of Profits*. Cambridge: Cambridge University Press.

Yasui, Shuji. (1969). "Keynes' Theory of Distribution: A Restatement and Some Extensions."* *Economic Studies Quarterly* (Journal of the Japanese Association of Theoretical Economics) 20(2), 16–26.

Young, Allyn A. (1928). "Increasing Returns and Economic Progress." *Economic Journal* 38, 527–542.

INDEX